W9-BFI-284

Tupac Shakur

Other books in the People in the News series:

Beyoncé
Jamie Foxx
Angelina Jolie
Ashton Kutcher
Avril Lavigne
Tobey Maguire
Barack Obama
J.K. Rowling
Hilary Swank

people
in the NEWS

J
B
SHA

Tupac Shakur

by **Michael V. Uschan**

LUCENT BOOKS

An imprint of Thomson Gale, a part of The Thomson Corporation

THOMSON
—— ✴ ——™
GALE

Detroit • New York • San Francisco
New Haven, Conn. • Waterville, Maine • London

Ing. 33.00 3-10

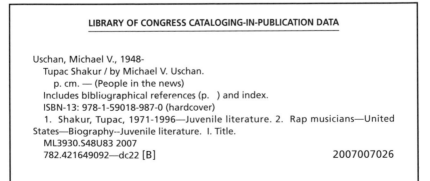

LIBRARY OF CONGRESS CATALOGING-IN-PUBLICATION DATA

Uschan, Michael V., 1948-
  Tupac Shakur / by Michael V. Uschan.
    p. cm. — (People in the news)
  Includes bibliographical references (p.) and index.
  ISBN-13: 978-1-59018-987-0 (hardcover)
    1. Shakur, Tupac, 1971-1996—Juvenile literature. 2. Rap musicians—United States—Biography--Juvenile literature. I. Title.
  ML3930.S48U83 2007
  782.421649092—dc22 [B]   2007007026

ISBN 10: 1-59018-987-6
Printed in the United States of America

Contents

F ame and celebrity are alluring. People are drawn to those who walk in fame's spotlight, whether they are known for great accomplishments or for notorious deeds. The lives of the famous pique public interest and attract attention, perhaps because their experiences seem in some ways so different from, yet in other ways so similar to, our own.

Newspapers, magazines, and television regularly capitalize on this fascination with celebrity by running profiles of famous people. For example, television programs such as *Entertainment Tonight* devote all of their programming to stories about entertainment and entertainers. Magazines such as *People* fill their pages with stories of the private lives of famous people. Even newspapers, newsmagazines, and television news frequently delve into the lives of well-known personalities. Despite the number of articles and programs, few provide more than a superficial glimpse at their subjects.

Lucent's People in the News series offers young readers a deeper look into the lives of today's newsmakers, the influences that have shaped them, and the impact they have had in their fields of endeavor and on other people's lives. The subjects of the series hail from many disciplines and walks of life. They include authors, musicians, athletes, political leaders, entertainers, entrepreneurs, and others who have made a mark on modern life and who, in many cases, will continue to do so for years to come.

These biographies are more than factual chronicles. Each book emphasizes the contributions, accomplishments, or deeds that have brought fame or notoriety to the individual and shows how that person has influenced modern life. Authors portray their subjects in a realistic, unsentimental light. For example, Bill Gates—the cofounder and chief executive officer of the software giant Microsoft—has been instrumental in making personal computers the most vital tool of the modern age. Few dispute his business savvy, his perseverance, or his technical expertise, yet critics say he is ruthless in his dealings with competitors and driven more by his desire to maintain Microsoft's dominance in the computer industry than by an interest in furthering technology.

In these books, young readers will encounter inspiring stories about real people who achieved success despite enormous obstacles. Oprah Winfrey—the most powerful, most watched, and wealthiest woman on television today—spent the first six years of her life in the care of her grandparents while her unwed mother sought work and a better life elsewhere. Her adolescence was colored by promiscuity, pregnancy at age fourteen, rape, and sexual abuse.

Each author documents and supports his or her work with an array of primary and secondary source quotations taken from diaries, letters, speeches, and interviews. All quotes are footnoted to show readers exactly how and where biographers derive their information and provide guidance for further research. The quotations enliven the text by giving readers eyewitness views of the life and accomplishments of each person covered in the People in the News series.

In addition, each book in the series includes photographs, annotated bibliographies, timelines, and comprehensive indexes. For both the casual reader and the student researcher, the People in the News series offers insight into the lives of today's newsmakers—people who shape the way we live, work, and play in the modern age.

More than a Rapper

When people hear the name Tupac Shakur, they probably visualize a bald-headed, handsome young man whose muscular upper body is vividly decorated with tattoos. The most prominent tattoo spreads in a graceful arc across his abdomen, its outlined letters reading "THUG LIFE." This imagined Tupac is most likely posing in an aggressive stance, his eyes glaring, his mouth twisted downward in a bitter frown, his hand raised in an obscene gesture.

That is the way almost everyone remembers Tupac, who died on September 13, 1996, six days after he was shot in Las Vegas, Nevada. That image sums up the anger, violence, and rebellion that were the essence of his songs and the personality he presented to the public. Those same elements were also a part of his own life, often tragically. Tupac was involved in several shooting incidents, arrested many times, and served eight months in prison. Yet this multitalented creative artist once visualized himself in a far different way. In a poem he wrote, Tupac once compared himself to a fragile flower fighting for life in the midst of a decaying city. The poem begins "Did u hear about the rose that grew from a crack in the concrete."[1]

The poem's title— "The Rose That Grew from Concrete"—became the title of his first book of poetry. The metaphor of the rose struggling to grow from cracked concrete in the city instead of in a well-tended garden symbolized Tupac's fight to survive the poverty, violence, and racism that haunted his youth so he could realize his dreams of becoming rich and famous.

The words reveal Tupac's gentle, introspective side. That they were in a poem and not a rap song laced with expletives is evidence that his creative drive took many forms.

Tupac Shakur and recording artist Janet Jackson starred in the 1993 movie Poetic Justice.

An Artist of Many Talents

Although he lived only twenty-five years, Tupac filled that quarter century with a long list of achievements as a rapper, poet, and actor. All those areas of artistic endeavor involve words, either written or spoken. His mother, Afeni Shakur, claims her son had a lifelong love affair with words: "Tupac loved to read! Books were a constant part of his life. As much as Tupac loved to read, he enjoyed talking."[2]

Tupac expressed his love of the written word in two books of poetry. The poems were written between 1989 and 1991, several years before he became famous, and they reflect a more gentle side of his personality than do many of his rap songs. The poems are infused with the anger and shame Tupac felt in growing up poor and black, emotions that would become the most powerful element of his rap lyrics. However, Tupac's poems also express how much he loved people in his life, from girls he dated to his mother and even a white high school buddy. And whether Tupac was describing the hardships of ghetto life or the joys of his personal relationships, the words he chose had the power to convey exactly how he felt. Afeni believes her son's skill with words was his greatest talent. In a preface to *The Rose That Grew from Concrete*, she wrote:

> There was never a day when Tupac did not appreciate language. The sound and the rhythm of words did not intimidate him. He sought to interpret his world using all the visual and linguistic tools available to him. They were the heart and soul of my son. They represent the process of a young artist's journey to understand and accept a world of unthinkable contradictions.[3]

As a rapper, Tupac employed other skills to make his songs come alive. In singing and talking the lyrics, he used his voice to inject even more bitterness, anger, and hatred into the words he had penned. The facial expressions, gestures, and dance movements that Tupac choreographed for his stage shows and videos helped him explain the story his songs told and communicate the messages he embedded in them. Even the array of

Tupac Shakur, known best as a tough gangsta rapper, loved to read books and write poetry.

tattoos that covered his body and the clothes he wore, from torn shirts to knotted bandannas around his head, helped him communicate with his fans by showing that he was like them.

Tupac also transposed into acting the verbal and physical skills that made his songs so dramatic. On January 17, 1992, two months after his first album, *2Pacalypse Now*, was released, Tupac's first movie opened in theaters. In *Juice*, Tupac earned rave reviews for his performance as Bishop, a violent young man who hated the world. Later he appeared in a half-dozen other films, including *Poetic Justice* with Janet Jackson. He also made several television appearances. A memorable one was an episode of *A Different World* in which he played the boyfriend of actress Jada Pinkett Smith, a close friend from his high school days.

But Tupac always considered himself more than an entertainer. He believed that his poetry, acting, and rapping were simply methods to achieve a higher goal, which was to criticize and change the social and economic conditions that made life hard for so many African Americans.

Tupac the Crusader

Tupac once explained his role as a crusader by comparing himself to reporters and photographers who had covered the Vietnam War. He said the stories and photographs they produced helped end the war by showing Americans how brutal the conflict really was. Tupac wanted to do the same thing in exposing injustices that blacks faced:

> So I thought, that's what I'm going to do as an artist, as a rapper. I'm gonna show the most graphic details of what I see in my community and hopefully they'll stop it quick. I've seen all of that—the crack babies, what we had to go through, losing everything, being poor, and getting beat down. All of that. Being the person I am I said no no no no. I'm changing this.[4]

His work contained powerful statements about issues blacks had to deal with. However, many people ignored his message because of the obscenities his songs contained and because his own lifestyle made him seem part of the problem he was describing.

Chapter 1

Tupac Shakur's Revolutionary Heritage

"**G**angsta rap" is a genre of hip-hop music that focuses on the lifestyles of gang members who live in the inner city. Its songs often glorify and condone violence, drug use, and criminal activity, including murdering police officers. Gangsta rappers work hard to project a bad-guy image in their performances and personal life so their fans will consider them as tough as the characters they sing about. Many rappers have engaged in gang activities and some have even served time in prison for crimes they have committed. No rapper, however, had a greater claim to having been bad from birth than Tupac Shakur. He announced with great pride, "My mother was pregnant with me while she was in prison. A month after she got outta prison she gave birth to me. So I was cultivated in prison, my embryo was in prison."[5]

That boast provided Tupac with an authenticity of toughness no other rapper could rival. More importantly, however, the reason Tupac's mother had been imprisoned during her pregnancy was a key factor in shaping his childhood and instilling in him some of the most important beliefs that he would hold throughout his life.

Tupac's Black Panther Heritage

Afeni Tupac was born Alice Faye Williams in Lumberton, North Carolina, in 1947. Her family moved to New York when she was eleven. At the age of eighteen she changed her first name to Afeni to show pride in her African heritage. She also joined the Black Panther party, a militant, radical group that was created in California in 1966 to fight racism and help African Americans have a better life. In big cities like New York, Chicago, and San Francisco, the Panthers created social programs that helped poor blacks, but some members engaged in violent acts and committed crimes to get money for party activities.

In September 1968, Afeni married Lumumba Shakur, a Panther leader. Several months later, on April 2, 1969, she and twenty other party members were arrested on charges of conspiring to destroy property by blowing up buildings and killing white people. Afeni described how she and other Panthers were

Afeni Shakur, center, and Lumumba Shakur, right, after their April 1969 arrest in connection with a Black Panther bombing plot.

The Black Panthers

The Black Panther party was started in Oakland, California, in October 1966 by Huey P. Newton and Bobby Seale. It was one of many organizations in the 1960s that fought for black civil rights. The Panthers were militant about defending blacks from racist violence, and members armed themselves with guns. The Panthers operated food kitchens and medical clinics in many communities, but the good things they did were often overshadowed by criminal acts and violent incidents, including gun battles with police. The Panthers helped blacks become proud of themselves and gave them hope for a better future. Afeni Shakur became aware of the Black Panthers when she heard Seale give a speech in Harlem, New York. Seale's message made her proud of herself and inspired her to fight for black rights. In a biography written by Jasmine Guy, Afeni explained what the Panthers did for her: "They educated my mind and gave me direction. With that direction came hope, and I loved them for giving me that. Because I never had hope in my life."

Jasmine Guy, *Afeni Shakur: Evolution of a Revolutionary*. New York: Atria, 2004, p. 62.

arrested: "The police burst in and put shotguns to our heads and stomachs. Children were in the apartment and they pointed shotguns at them as well."[6] She and the other defendants in the case became known as the Panther 21. Afeni was released on bail in January 1970 after a fund-raising effort by whites and blacks who supported the Panthers. In February 1971, when two of the Panther 21 failed to show up for a court appearance, she and other defendants were sent back to jail because officials feared they would also flee to avoid trial. Afeni, who was pregnant, remained in jail until May 13, 1971, when she and the other Panthers were acquitted of all charges. She played an important role in the acquittal by acting as her own lawyer. Even though she had dropped out of school after eleventh grade, Afeni was brilliant in cross-examining police officers to prove she had done nothing wrong. She also influenced jurors in her powerful closing argument when she told them: "Do what you have to do. All we ask of you is that you judge us fairly. Please judge us according to the way that you want to be judged."[7]

On June 16, 1971, thirty-four days after Afeni was found innocent, Tupac was born in the East Harlem section of New York City. Afeni originally named him Parish Lesane Crooks because she feared someone would hurt him because of her radical activities. A year later she gave him the name he would make famous—Tupac Amaru Shakur. Tupac Amaru was the name of an Inca warrior who led an uprising in Peru against Spain—his name in Quechua means "Shining Serpent." *Shakur* is the Arabic word for "thankful to God." Tupac's new name reflected the revolutionary heritage his mother wanted him to embrace.

Tupac's Childhood

Tupac's father was also a Black Panther. Billy Garland had met Afeni while she was out on bail. Although he was Tupac's biological father, he never helped raise his son. Afeni, who had divorced Lumumba Shakur, worked as a paralegal to support herself and Tupac. She cherished education and believed it was important for Tupac to learn to think independently. "I knew I was raising a young black man in a society that kills young black men, and that his best weapon would be a strong, brilliant, and agile mind," she said.[8] In addition to sending Tupac to preschool and then public school, she also enrolled him in creative workshops for dancing, singing, and writing.

Afeni's drive to educate Tupac in the arts included enrolling him in the 127th Street Ensemble, an acclaimed theater group in Harlem, a black neighborhood in New York. He studied acting with the group and when he was twelve appeared in *A Raisin in the Sun*, a famous play about racism. The cast performed the play at the Apollo Theater, a legendary Harlem venue for black artists. The experience was one of the most powerful in Tupac's childhood because it gave him confidence in himself and a chance to escape, at least for a while, from the often bitter reality of his life. He said, "This is something that none of them

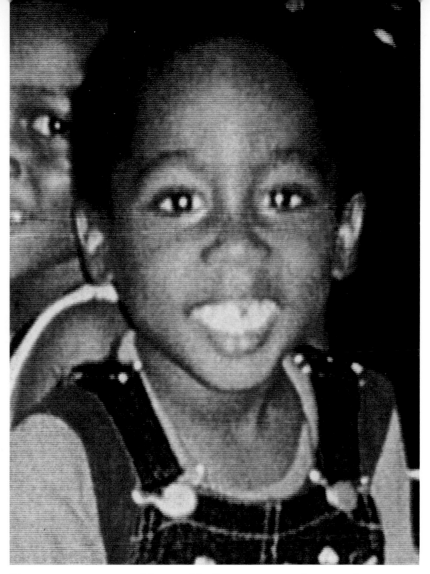

From a young age, Tupac Shakur was taught to value education, both in school and in the arts.

[other] kids can do. I didn't like my life, but through acting, I could become somebody else."[9]

One reason Tupac did not like his life was that he did not know his biological father and had no permanent father figure in his life. The closest person to a real dad that Tupac had was Mutulu Shakur, a Black Panther who fathered Tupac's stepsister Sekyiwa. Shakur was not in Tupac's life long because he went to prison in 1981 for robbing an armored truck and killing two guards. Tupac admitted years later that the lack of a father made him sad and pushed him into a world of fantasy:

I never knew where my father was or who my father was for sure. [When] I was young I was quiet, withdrawn. I read a lot, wrote poetry, kept a diary. I watched TV all day. I stayed in front of the television. I thought if I could be and act like those characters, act like those people, I could have some of their joy. If I could act like I had a big family I wouldn't feel as lonely.[10]

Afeni was released from her job with South Bronx Legal Services because of her connection to Mutulu, a convicted felon.

Growing Up Without a Father

Tupac Shakur was one of many black children who had to grow up without a father. Billy Garland, his biological father, was never around when Tupac was growing up. Mutulu Shakur, his mother's boyfriend, was an important figure in Tupac's life for a short period, and Tupac was grateful to him for the time he spent with a young boy who longed for a father. But even Mutulu was only in Tupac's life for a few years because he went to prison in 1988 for robbing an armored truck. Tupac deeply missed having a father and recognized what the lack meant in his life:

I hate saying this cuz white people love hearing black people talking about this. But I know for a fact that had I had a father, I'd have some discipline. I'd have more confidence. Your mother cannot calm you down the way a man can. Your mother can't reassure you the way a man can. My mother couldn't show me where my manhood was. You need a man to teach you how to be a man.

Jacob Hoye and Karolyn Ali, eds., *Tupac: Resurrection, 1971–1996.* New York: Atria, 2003, p. 24.

A scene from the 1954 version of A Raisin in the Sun, *starring Ruby Dee, Sydney Poitier, and Diana Sands.*

Unemployed and without any money, she could no longer afford her apartment and had to live with her sister, Gloria Cox. In June 1986, when Tupac was thirteen years old, Afeni decided to move her family to Baltimore so she could start a new life.

A New Life in Baltimore

Tupac had to move many times during his childhood, but this move was one of the best things that ever happened to him. In New York, Afeni had not only worked as a paralegal but also

As a twelve-year-old, Tupac Shakur's first acting experience took place at the legendary Apollo Theater in Harlem, New York City.

remained active with the Black Panthers. She was often chosen to make speeches because of her fame from the Panther 21 trial. Tupac had always been proud of her because she had gained so much respect as a Panther: "Everybody else's mother was just a regular mother, but my mother was Afeni—you know what I'm saying?"[11] But Tupac had also been jealous because she spent so much time away from home helping other people. In Baltimore, Afeni was able to spend more time with her children, and Tupac relished his new, closer relationship with her.

Afeni was on welfare when she moved to Baltimore, but after taking computer training she worked as a data processor. Tupac attended Roland Park Middle School and then Paul Lawrence Dunbar High School for his freshman year. But then, in what he claimed was one of the luckiest breaks of his life, he was accepted by the Baltimore School of the Arts. This public high school is nationally known for training students in the visual arts, music, theater, and dance. Tupac studied acting, jazz, and ballet. He also developed a love for the plays of William Shakespeare.

A New School with New Friends

Tupac also had another new, important educational experience at the school. Because it was integrated, he became friendly for the first time with white classmates like John Cole. He even wrote a poem about him called "White Boy John." Said Tupac of learning to socialize with whites, "That was the first time I saw that there were white people you could get along with. Before that, I just believed what everyone else said, that they was devils. But I loved it. I loved going to school. It taught me a lot. I was really starting to feel like I really wanted to be an artist."[12]

Tupac also had many black friends, including Jada Pinkett, who became an actress and later married rapper and actor Will Smith. Tupac and Jada were very close and performed together in school plays. In a poem titled "Jada," Tupac referred to her as the "omega of my Heart."[13]

Writing poems was only one way Tupac was expressing himself in this period. He also began writing rap songs.

Tupac Becomes MC New York

Tupac's flair for entertaining and his skill with words made it easy for him to perform rap songs at parties. He would pick up the microphone, make up some lyrics, and sing just to have a good time. Because he was from New York, he became known as MC (Master of Ceremonies) New York. He quickly gained a local reputation as a talented young rapper.

In rap, the teenager found an art form that gave him a powerful new outlet for his creativity as well as a sense of pride because he did it so well. Tupac claimed that "it brought me to myself."[14] Tupac liked rap music because it seemed more exciting than other styles that were popular then and because the

Tupac Shakur's mother, Afeni, remained active with the Black Panthers during Tupac's childhood.

A Lesson from His Mom

In this excerpt from the book *Tupac Shakur Legacy*, author Jamal Joseph describes how Tupac's mother taught him not to be ashamed of being poor.

Afeni [Shakur] recalls a day when Tupac came home angry and embarrassed by his secondhand clothes. He was being teased in school; kids with new sneakers and Kangol hats were calling him a bum. It was the first time Tupac lashed out at his mother about being poor. Inspired by the Roberta Flack song "Go Up Moses," Afeni took three shiny pennies from her purse and a crumpled hundred-dollar bill and put them on the table. She asked her son to choose one. Tupac chose the bill over the pennies. Afeni explained to him that he took the bill despite its outward appearance because he saw its true value and wasn't fooled by the shine. She went on to explain that self-worth and developing the best *within* was far more valuable than any exterior. Moved by his mother's words, Tupac took a pair of old jeans and a denim jacket, cut them up, and added graffiti art and an "MC New York" logo. He not only got compliments on his clothes, he started a trend.

Jamal Joseph, *Tupac Shakur Legacy*. New York: Atria, 2006, p. 17.

songs detailed the problems of poverty, racism, and crime that black people faced in their daily lives. He had heard his mother talk about those themes as a Panther, and that connection made rap more meaningful to him than other types of music. That serious side of his nature led him to organize an antigun youth rally after a friend was shot to death. He sang a rap song at the event that opposed violence and guns.

Even though he was becoming a popular rapper, Tupac remained serious about his studies. In addition to working hard in his classes, Tupac devoured many books because he wanted to keep learning new things. He read everything from books on Eastern religion to sets of encyclopedias.

His own life was not without its problems. The main one was that his family did not have much money. Tupac resented not being able to buy nice clothes and other things he wanted. "I hated growing up poor, and it made me very bitter," he admitted years later.[15] One reason for his family's financial problems was that his mother was becoming addicted to drugs.

Problems and Another Move

When Afeni was living in New York, she had sometimes used cocaine, marijuana, and LSD, but she had never become addicted to those drugs. After moving to Baltimore, Afeni became hooked on a more dangerous drug—crack cocaine. As her crack habit grew, her family's home life deteriorated.

In an interview Afeni once said of those days, "There was no stability. I was smoking and screwing up my life."[16] One way she did that was in the choice of the men she brought into her life, including one who hit her while living with her. When Tupac wanted to retaliate against the man, she talked him out of it. Said Afeni, "Tupac wanted to beat [him up], and I made him promise not to beat up the man. Tupac was sixteen at this time and never forgave me for not letting him protect me."[17]

In an effort to escape her addiction and better the lives of her children, Afeni decided to move her family to California. In June 1988 she sent Tupac and Sekyiwa to live with a friend in Marin County, California. Afeni planned to join them when she had saved some money, but in October her friend announced that she was going to enter a drug and alcohol rehabilitation center. She said that if Afeni did not get there right away, her children would be placed in a foster home. Afeni sold everything she had and took a bus to California to be with her children.

"I Was Lonely"

The move across the continent was the longest Tupac made while growing up. However, it was only one of many. In New York his mother had changed apartments frequently and they had lived in several places in Baltimore; sometimes, in both cities, their residence was a homeless shelter. Tupac admitted that the constant moving made his childhood difficult: "I remember crying all the time. My major thing growing up was I couldn't fit in. Because I was from everywhere. Every time I had to go to a new apartment, I had to reinvent myself. I was lonely."[18]

In California, Tupac would finally fit in. He would do it by becoming a successful rapper.

2Pacalypse Now Hits the World

At first Tupac Shakur thought that the move to California in 1988 was one of the worst things that had ever happened to him. He had loved the Baltimore School of the Arts and wanted to finish high school there. Years later he admitted, "Leaving that school affected me so much. Even now, I see that as the point where I got off track."[19] Tupac's life fell apart during his first few years in California—he dropped out of school, was homeless much of the time, and had to work a variety of odd jobs to support himself.

But even during one of the hardest periods of his life, Tupac never gave up his dream of becoming a rich and famous rapper. And because Tupac never lost that faith, the move to California eventually became the best thing that ever happened to him.

Tupac Becomes a Panther

After racing across the country by bus to be with her children, Afeni moved her family into a housing project located in a tough part of Marin City known as "the Jungle." Tupac began his junior year at Tamalpais High School but soon dropped out; he later earned a general equivalency degree.

One reason Tupac quit school is that he did not think he was learning anything meaningful. He had enjoyed his classes in Baltimore because he believed they were preparing him for a career in the arts, but that was not true of his courses at Tamal-

For a while before he became a superstar, Tupac Shakur was homeless and broke. Yet he never quit working toward his goal of becoming a rapper.

pais. Tupac explained once why school curriculums need to be meaningful to students: "I like to think of myself as socially aware. I think there should be a drug class, a sex education class. A class on police brutality. There should be a class on apartheid. There should be a class on why people are hungry, but there are not. There are classes on . . . gym. Physical education. Let's learn volleyball."[20]

Tupac found an outlet for his concerns about social problems in the black community by becoming a leader of the New Afrikan Panthers (NAP). Like the Black Panther party of his parents, NAP fought against racism, poverty, and police brutality. Tupac became a spokesman for the group's young members. In a radio interview in 1989 he said, "I believe that the New Afrikan Panthers are about serious freedom . . . and serious liberation and self-determination." Tupac already had a name that represented his African roots, and he advised other blacks to choose names that showed pride in their heritage. But he also said that a new name was not enough: "Don't just get an African name—get an African brain. Don't walk around with the name if you can't defend the ideals [of African heritage] and if you don't even know your culture."[21]

But even while Tupac was trying to help other blacks deal with problems associated with poverty and racism, his own mother was falling victim to one—drug addiction. Her increasing use of crack cocaine was a blow to a son who loved his mother deeply. "After she started smoking dope and all that, I, like, lost respect for her," Tupac said. "In New York and all those times we was growing up, she was my hero."[22] Unable to stand seeing his mother destroy herself, Tupac left home to begin his own life not long after arriving in California.

Tupac Struggles

Tupac, who had always lived in poverty, was now homeless and broke. To support himself, he took many types of jobs, including working in a pizza parlor. He was forced at times to live off the charity of friends who let him sleep at their homes, fed him, and even gave him money to survive. Many of his new acquaintances were gang members, drug dealers, and pimps. Tupac later claimed that these people were the only ones who cared about him during this period. In order to survive, Tupac tried selling drugs but quit after a short time because he was no good at it. He explained how he failed at this illegal enterprise:

> I tried selling drugs for maybe like two weeks. And then the dude [who gave him the drugs] was like, "Oh man, give me my drugs back," cuz I didn't know how to do it. Then the dope dealers used to look out for me. They would just give me money and be like, "Don't get involved in this, get out there and do your dream." So they were like my sponsors.[23]

Even when he had to sleep in homeless shelters, Tupac never quit working toward his goal of becoming a rapper. At parties he would grab the microphone and start rapping, even though it sometimes annoyed other people. He also continued writing poetry and other pieces that would later become the basis for many of his rap songs. The stories and portraits of life that Tupac wrote down came directly from his observations of people and events in his daily life. As his mother said, "When he got to Marin City, Tupac was taught the streets."[24] Those experiences would help make his songs popular by giving them a gritty realism.

It was during this period that he wrote "The Rose That Grew from Concrete." Strangely, Tupac's love of poetry led to an opportunity that would begin his rap career.

Becoming a Rapper

In the spring of 1989 Tupac met Leila Steinberg, a poet, teacher, and musical talent agent. Steinberg was sitting outside Bayside Elementary School in Marin City reading *Part of My Soul Went with Him* by Winnie Mandela when Tupac walked by. Noticing the title of the book Steinberg was holding, he began quoting from it. "It fascinated me that he knew the lines by heart," said Steinberg.[25] After they talked for a while, she invited Tupac to join the poetry group she led.

The meeting was important because Steinberg became his first agent. Tupac's efforts as a rapper had not been very successful even though he was rapping every chance he got; he even lived with Steinberg's family for a while because he was so poor. Tupac had teamed up with a friend called DJ Dize—pronounced "dizzy"—to form the group Strictly Dope. The duo made some low-budget recordings of their songs, which were released in 2001 as *Tupac Shakur: The Lost Tapes*. But the big break Tupac needed to sign a recording contract or join a major group had eluded him until he met Steinberg.

With Steinberg's help, Strictly Dope was invited to perform at the 1989 Marin City Festival. Tupac did so well himself that Steinberg managed to get him a tryout with the rap group Digital Underground. Greg Jacobs, the group's lead singer, was known as "Shock G." He liked Tupac and hired him as a dancer

Touring with Digital Underground was Tupac Shakur's first big break in the music industry.

and roadie, a person who sets up stage equipment and does other odd jobs. In 1990 Tupac toured with Digital Underground in the United States and Japan.

Although Tupac was not yet a star in his own right, he made enough money to rent an apartment, buy a car, and give money to his mother, who was still struggling with drugs. In January 1991 Tupac made his recording debut by singing one of the verses of "Same Song," a tune on Digital Underground's *This Is an EP Release* (the tapes he and friends made were only distributed locally originally). He also appeared in the song's music video. The lyrics he sang included "Now I clown around when I hang around with the Underground."[26] Tupac also boasted in that song that women who once ignored him were now eager to date him, which was true because he was becoming a well-known celebrity.

The song became a big hit and, just like the lines he sang, Tupac began to be recognized by fans. His success with the group only whetted his appetite for what he really wanted—to be famous on his own. "That was my number-one thing when I first got in the business. Everybody's gonna know me," he said.[27] To achieve that goal, Tupac knew he had to have a solo album. He would get his wish with *2Pacalypse Now*.

The "2Pacalypse" Arrives

It is not easy for a young performer to win a contract with a record company. Tupac was lucky because he got help from Anton Gregory, who managed Digital Underground. Gregory convinced Interscope Records to give the young rapper a chance. The company signed him and on November 12, 1991, just ten months after his recording debut with Digital Underground, *2Pacalypse Now* was released.

The album title was a sly variation on his name and the word *apocalypse*, a biblical term that signifies the time when the world will end after a final battle between good and evil. The title was not only clever but indicated the serious nature of the album's songs. Digital Underground was known for fun-loving, sexy songs that people played at parties, but the lyrical content of *2Pacalypse Now* was much edgier and harsher. Its songs dealt with the grim reality of life in black inner cities. Asked in an interview what the album was about, Tupac replied, "Police brutality, poverty, unemployment, insufficient education, disunity and violence, black on black crime, teenage pregnancy, crack addiction. Do you want me to go on?"[28]

Many of the songs became controversial because the stories they told seemed brutal even though they were a true reflection of inner-city life. One of the album's biggest hits was "Brenda's Got a Baby," about a twelve-year-old girl who ruins her life by becoming pregnant. Brenda never knew her mother and her father died of heroin addiction. The song explains how she confuses sex with love and thinks her teenage lover will help her

A Radio Interview with Tupac Shakur

In 1991, Tupac was interviewed on San Francisco radio station KMEL by David Cook, a disc jockey whose on-air name was "Davey D." Tupac talked about the underlying theme of *2Pacalypse Now*:

> The concept is the young Black male. Everybody's been talkin' about it but now it's not important. It's like we just skipped over it. It's no longer a fad to be down for the young Black male. Everybody wants to go past. Like the gangster stuff, it just got exploited. This was just like back in the days with the movies. Everybody did their little gunshots and their hand grenades and blew up stuff and moved on. Now everybody's doing rap songs with the singing in it. I'm still down for the young Black male. I'm gonna stay until things get better. So it's all about addressing the problems that we face in everyday society.

"Tupac Shakur Speaks." Interviews on a CD accompanying the book *Tupac Shakur Legacy* by Jamal Joseph. New York: Atria, 2006.

Strong stage presence and emotional lyrics made Tupac Shakur a star almost immediately upon release of his first album, 2Pacalypse Now.

with the baby, only to have him leave her. After Brenda gives birth, she throws the baby away in the trash.

Tupac was criticized for being negative about women by mocking Brenda's plight—one line in the song says that Brenda might have a baby but only barely had a brain. However, Tupac wrote the song to wake up people, both black and white, to the damage done by teenage pregnancy not only to young women but to the black community as a whole. None of his critics ever mentioned this line from that song: "Just cause your in tha ghetto doesn't mean ya can't grow."[29] Tupac was arguing that the girl's horrible childhood was no excuse for the mistakes she made and that she should have tried harder to change her life for the better.

The song expressed the terrible things that were happening to young blacks. Tupac was able to write powerfully about such events because he understood them from his own personal experience.

"My Songs Deal with Pain"

Part of Tupac's success as a rapper was that he was handsome and had a dramatic stage presence. The most powerful appeal of his songs, however, was the emotional stories they told about the tough times real inner-city residents were experiencing. His rough take on black life shocked many people. But Tupac always said he wrote his songs from his heart, a heart he claimed was filled with the pain of living: "All my songs deal with pain. That's what makes me *me*. That's what makes me do what I do. Everything is based on the pain I felt in my childhood. Small pieces of it and harsh pieces of it."[30]

Some of that pain occurred during his early years in California. He hated watching his mother descend into addiction and he struggled at times to find a place to sleep and get enough money to buy food. His failure to sell drugs and his abject poverty in this period made Tupac the butt of jokes by some blacks who thought he was a loser. Yet as he became successful as a rapper, Tupac for the first time in his life began to feel comfortable and accepted. "It was like a 'hood and I wanted to be a part of it. If I could just fit in here, I'm cool. And I thought

I did," he said.[31] That sense of belonging was so powerful that he refused to cut himself off from such people even after he became rich and famous.

An Overnight Superstar

The success of Tupac's first album catapulted him instantly into stardom. Years later, he noted that even he was surprised at how fast it happened. Until the release of *2Pacalypse Now*, Tupac was a minor member of Digital Underground whose duties included dancing occasionally with an inflatable female doll to the group's hit song "The Humpty Dance." The performance was degrading

Tupac's Love for His Mother

Tupac began writing poetry as a young boy. He wrote many poems between 1989 and 1991, when he was struggling to survive in California and become a successful rapper. In one poem published after his death in *The Rose That Grew from Concrete*, Tupac explains the pain he felt about his mother's drug addiction. The poem is titled "When Ure Hero Falls 4 My Hero (My Mother)." It is a touching tribute to the great love Tupac felt for his mother even though she hurt him by becoming a crack addict. Tupac notes the great pain he experienced at seeing that his mother, like all addicts, was too weak to overcome her need for a drug. That deeply hurt Tupac because his mother had always been a source of strength in his life; she had, indeed, been his hero, especially because his father was never around to help raise him. As Tupac asks in the poem, "what R u expected 2 do when ure only Hero falls." Her addiction taught him the bitter lesson that even heroes can have flaws.

Tupac Amaru Shakur, *The Rose That Grew from Concrete*. New York: Pocket, 1999, p. 119.

Tupac Shakur and Patrick Henry

One of the American Revolution's most famous quotes is "Give me liberty or give me death," spoken by Virginia legislator Patrick Henry in 1775 while arguing that the colonists had to fight England to win their freedom. Tupac used those words as the title of a 1992 essay in which he compared patriots like Henry to black youths fighting for independence in a white-dominated world. The struggle of blacks for freedom from racism and poverty was the focus of many of Tupac's rap songs. He wrote:

> As a Jr. High student reading about the period of the American Revolution I understood what Patrick Henry meant when he uttered those words. I think every black male and minority youth in general can relate greatly to that [and] I never forgot who Patrick Henry was because even as a youngster I understood his thirst for liberty; and now as a young black man coming of age in a world who promises my extinction before the turn of the century, I too want to cry out those same words.

Jamal Joseph, *Tupac Shakur Legacy*. New York: Atria, 2006, p. 8.

for someone who wanted to become a star, but Tupac knew it was one way to achieve what he wanted. After he became successful, he joked, "So I went from dancing [nearly] naked with dolls, being unknown, to having a platinum record."[32] After that first album became a hit, Tupac Shakur would never be unknown again.

Chapter 3

Tupac Becomes a Superstar

Tupac Shakur never felt that he fit in anywhere during his childhood and teenage years. But his success as a rapper finally made him feel accepted; he even boasted that he would be recognized and warmly welcomed by his fans in any city across the nation. Success, however, transformed Tupac in an even more important way: "Being famous and having money gave me confidence," he said. "The screams of the crowd gave me confidence. Before that I was a shell of a man. Now I believe that I'm my own man."[33]

He made that statement during an interview to promote not only his first album but also *Juice*, a movie that debuted in theaters on January 17, 1992. Tupac's extraordinary creative talents were quickly making him the rarest of entertainers—a star in both music and films. He was able to do it by working very hard.

Thug Life

2Pacalypse Now made Tupac a star, but he was so busy touring to perform for his fans and making films that he did not release his second album until February 1, 1993. Titled *Strictly 4 My N.I.G.G.A.Z.*, it had two hit singles—"Keep Ya Head Up" and "I Get Around." The album sold more copies than his first and made Tupac the leading figure in a new genre of hip-hop music called "gangsta rap" because its songs glorified the lifestyle of inner-city gang members. Like *2Pacalypse Now*, Tupac's second album was controversial. Its songs offended many people because of their obscene language, violent themes, approval of drug use and criminal activity, and a demeaning attitude toward women.

Tupac made an even bigger impact on gangsta rap on September 24, 1994, with the release of *Thug Life Vol. 1*. Thug Life was the name of the group of singers and musicians Tupac had

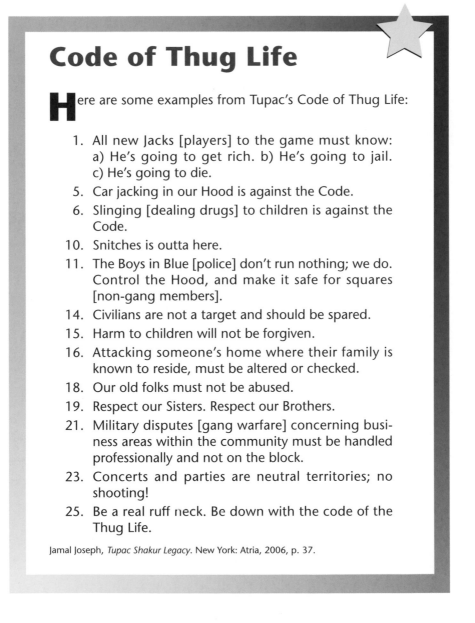

Code of Thug Life

Here are some examples from Tupac's Code of Thug Life:

1. All new Jacks [players] to the game must know: a) He's going to get rich. b) He's going to jail. c) He's going to die.
5. Car jacking in our Hood is against the Code.
6. Slinging [dealing drugs] to children is against the Code.
10. Snitches is outta here.
11. The Boys in Blue [police] don't run nothing; we do. Control the Hood, and make it safe for squares [non-gang members].
14. Civilians are not a target and should be spared.
15. Harm to children will not be forgiven.
16. Attacking someone's home where their family is known to reside, must be altered or checked.
18. Our old folks must not be abused.
19. Respect our Sisters. Respect our Brothers.
21. Military disputes [gang warfare] concerning business areas within the community must be handled professionally and not on the block.
23. Concerts and parties are neutral territories; no shooting!
25. Be a real ruff neck. Be down with the code of the Thug Life.

Jamal Joseph, *Tupac Shakur Legacy*. New York: Atria, 2006, p. 37.

assembled to record the album. Even more important, the phrase *thug life* represented Tupac's personal philosophy about the struggle black males faced while growing up with little hope for a decent life because of racism and poverty. The phrase was actually an acronym that summed up the social and economic disadvantages blacks faced. It stands for "The Hate U Gave Lil' Infants F— [hurts] Everyone." "Hate" was the embodiment of the factors that made life difficult for blacks from the moment they were born. This is how Tupac defined a thug:

> When I say thug I mean not a criminal, someone who beats you over the head. I mean the underdog. You could have two people—one person has everything he needs to suc-ceed and the other person has nothing. If the person who has nothing succeeds, he's a thug. Cuz he overcame all the obstacles. [It] doesn't have anything to do with the dictio-nary's version of thug. Sorry.[34]

Tupac even wrote a "Code of Thug Life" to show how people were supposed to behave. Several people helped him create these rules, including Mutulu Shakur, who was still in prison for robbing an armored bank truck. Among its twenty-six di-rectives were warnings that "thugs" did not shoot anyone at a party or concert, steal cars from people who lived in their neigh-borhood, sell drugs to children, or harm senior citizens.

Although Tupac claimed he was trying to give young blacks a positive message with *Thug Life*, critics blasted the violence, drug use, and sexual promiscuity its songs glorified. That criti-cism was nothing new for Tupac, who said repeatedly, "I didn't create thug life, I diagnosed it."[35]

The Furor over Tupac's Songs

One of Tupac's most controversial songs was on his first album. "Soulja's Story" is about a fifteen-year-old black youth who sells drugs. When the police try to arrest him, the youth fights back and kills one of the officers. The lyrics describe the shoot-ing: "They finally pull me over, and I laugh [and] I blast [the policeman]."[36]

The song upset many people when *2Pacalypse Now* was initially released because it made the teenage cop killer seem heroic. Anger over the lyrics exploded four months later when the song's fictional scenario became reality. On April 11, 1992, Texas state trooper Bill Davidson stopped twenty-year-old Ronald Ray Howard Sr. near Edna, Texas, after a high-speed chase because Howard was driving a stolen car. When Davidson approached the car, Howard shot the officer. Howard had been listening to "Soulja's Story" during the chase and he claimed that the song influenced him to kill the trooper. A jury convicted Howard, who was executed by lethal injection on October 6, 2005.

A Vice President Criticizes Tupac

The link between the song and an actual murder made many people condemn Tupac. His most famous critic was Vice President Dan Quayle, who on September 22, 1992, declared, "There's no reason for a record like this to be released. It has no place in our society."[37] Dennis R. Martin, a former president of the National Association of Chiefs of Police, was even harsher in his criticism of the song. Martin was, of course, angry about lyrics that portrayed killing a police officer as a heroic action. He was also shocked at the power of the new form of music called rap to sway the minds of young blacks who listened to it. In an article titled "The Music of Murder," he condemned "vile and dangerous lyrics" in many rap songs that could lead listeners to commit acts of violence. In commenting specifically on "Soulja's Story," Martin wrote:

> The teen-age killer, Ronald Howard, explained to law enforcement authorities that he felt hypnotized by the lyrics of [the song] which urged the killing of police officers. Howard claims that the lyrical instructions devoured him like an animal, taking control over his subconscious mind and compelling him to kill Trooper Davidson as he approached Howard's vehicle.[38]

Although the publicity generated by such negative comments made Tupac even more famous and popular, they failed to alter

Vice President Dan Quayle harshly criticized Tupac Shakur for glamorizing violent behavior and drug use in his rap songs.

the content of his lyrics. Songs in *Thug Life Vol. 1* once again made heroes out of violent criminals. "Bury Me a G" tells of a young man's wish to remain a gangster until he dies. The youth boasts that he has "just made 25 and I'm livin' like a savage."[39] In "Cradle to the Grave" the song's character advises young blacks to "be brave, and keep on thuggin', from the cradle to the grave."[40]

Filled with Rage

Tupac's critics were revolted that his songs praised violent behavior and sexual promiscuity and were laced with obscenities.

But by focusing on only those elements, they failed to note the powerful statements Tupac was making about the reality of life for poor blacks. The lyrics in Tupac's songs often dealt with important issues like drug addiction, gang violence, single mothers, men who fathered children but never parented them, racism, and the utter despair many young blacks felt about their future. Although his songs painted an ugly picture of black life, it was true in many ways. Tupac himself had suffered from poverty, his mother's addiction, and an absent father.

Tupac's critics, many of whom were white, could not comprehend the truths his songs contained because they had never experienced such conditions themselves. That made it hard for them to understand the anger and despair many blacks felt about their lives, like the youth in "Bury Me a G" who laments, "I got nothen' ta lose so I choose to be a killer."[41] Tupac once tried to explain why he believed his stark depiction of black life offended some people while making sense to young blacks:

> I make it [the truth of ghetto life] uncomfortable by putting details to it. It might not have been politically correct but I've reached somebody. [His fans are] relating to me. They related to the brutal honesty in the rap. And why shouldn't they be angry? And why shouldn't my raps that I'm rappin to my community be filled with rage?[42]

Tupac's Positive Message

Some of Tupac's songs contained positive messages such as advising blacks to fight racism and to stay hopeful about the future despite problems in their lives. Several songs praised black women and condemned black men for treating them shabbily. "Keep Ya Head Up" asks, "I wonder why we take from our women . . . do we hate our women?"[43] He said instead of mistreating black women, Tupac sings that it is time to treat them better. The song was his way of helping black women cope with the difficult lives many of them led.

Some of his songs praise black mothers, especially single mothers. "Dear Mama" is a loving, touching tribute to his own mother.

It contains one of the most memorable lines in rap: "Even though you was a crack fiend, mama, you still was a Black queen, mama."[44] "Dear Mama" became one of Tupac's biggest hits.

Although Tupac was praised for such positive messages about women, he was harshly criticized for demeaning women in many other songs. His lyrics regularly referred to women as "ho" (whore) and "bitch," often characterizing them as nothing more than willing sex partners. John McWhorter, an African American university professor, claims that "woman-bashing" was an essential part of many of Tupac's songs as well as the personality he projected while performing. McWhorter notes that even Tupac's powerful message about black women in "Keep Ya Head Up" is diluted by another song on the same album: "But the nobility of the sentiment is not allowed to stand unqualified. Just three tracks later comes 'I Get Around,' in which Shakur joins

Tupac Defends Black Women

Walter Edwards, a professor of linguistics at Wayne State University in Detroit, Michigan, believes Tupac was sensitive to the plight of poor African American women. Edwards writes: "In 'Part-time Mutha' he clearly sympathizes with the girl whose young dope-fiend mother was too preoccupied with her drug habit to take proper care of her daughter. The result is that her daughter was raped and made pregnant by her stepfather. Eventually the daughter had to tell her mother of the abuse only to be accused by her mother of seducing her rapist. Tupac's narrative is terse, clear and poetic. Here's the victim speaking: 'I grew up in a home where no one liked me.' The poem then recounts the frightening life the young girl led with a drug-addicted mother and a father who repeatedly raped her."

Walter Edwards, "From Poetry to Rap: The Lyrics of Tupac Shakur." *Western Journal of Black Studies* 26, no. 2 (2002): 67.

some guest rappers in telling women to stand in line, given that '2Pacalypse Now don't stop for no ho's.'"[45]

Despite Tupac's personal definition of thug life, his song lyrics often made him seem like the dictionary version of a thug. That image was also one that he portrayed convincingly in films.

Tupac the Actor

Tupac made a brief appearance as himself in the 1991 film *Nothing but Trouble*, but his first starring role was in *Juice*. The movie is about four black teenagers from Harlem who rob a grocery store to try to get "juice," a slang term for respect. Tupac played Roland Bishop. "It's a real good movie that happens to have hip hop [music] in it," he said about the film. "My character is a psychotic, insecure, very violent, very short-tempered individual."[46] Bishop shoots a store clerk during the robbery simply because he wants to kill someone. Despite Tupac's lack of acting

Tupac Shakur could relate to his role in the 1992 movie **Juice,** *which was about four inner-city teens pursuing power on the streets.*

Tupac's performance as a drug dealer in the 1994 film Above the Rim, *a scene from which is shown here, was praised by critics.*

experience, his portrayal of the gun-wielding teen was widely praised. It is considered his finest performance.

In *Above the Rim* in 1994, Tupac played Birdie, a drug dealer whose brother is a promising high school basketball player. His performance as a villain in both films was so convincing that it strengthened the public's belief that Tupac himself was a thug. However, Jeff Pollack, who directed *Above the Rim*, insisted that Tupac was believable because he was a good actor: "What allows Tupac to play bad guys so well is that he understands the anger and pain these people suffer. But he isn't that guy on the screen. He isn't a sociopathic killer. He's an actor. He builds his character with technique and craft."[47]

Tupac disproved his bad boy reputation in 1993's *Poetic Justice*, in which he starred opposite Janet Jackson. He gave a sensitive performance as Lucky, a thoughtful postal worker who writes poetry and is a loving father. Tupac again won rave reviews for his performance in the film.

He also acted on television. He appeared on shows featuring blacks like *In Living Color* and *A Different World*. On *A Different World* he was reunited with Jada Pinkett, his good friend from the Baltimore School of the Arts. In one episode he played Picolo, the boyfriend Pinkett's character left behind when she went to college and he did not. The story line mirrored their own separation when Tupac's family moved to California. The fact that the two friends were acting on a television show instead of a school play showed how much their lives had been

Jada Pinkett Smith and Tupac Shakur became close friends while both were students at the Baltimore School of the Arts.

Tupac Was "Lucky"

Tupac was famous for his roles as violent criminals like Bishop and Birdie. But he took great pride in playing Lucky in *Poetic Justice* because his character, a postal worker and loving father, showed that not all black men were gangsters. In an interview, Tupac said of the film:

All of our young black males are not violent, they're all not taking the law into their own hands. Lucky is doing it the opposite way that Bishop did. He's taking care of his daughter. He's a respectful person, you know what I'm saying? He lives in a home with his mother, he's not sweating it, that's where he wants to be. He wants to set goals and accomplish them. Lucky the Postman, that was me. I'm the type of person that could be a good father, a good homie, a good son, and a good man at the same time.

Jacob Hoye and Karolyn Ali, eds., *Tupac: Resurrection 1971–1996*. New York: Atria, 2003, p. 86.

transformed in just a few years. Tupac, however, became worried that success would alter his personality too much.

"I Didn't Want to Change"

By the time he was twenty-two, Tupac had released two successful albums and starred in two popular films. He loved the fame and money that his acting and singing had won him, but he was worried about becoming estranged from poor young blacks, who were not only his fans but the kind of people he had known all his life. To stay in touch with them, Tupac visited black inner-city neighborhoods and went to parties with people who were not celebrities. Said Tupac:

I didn't want to change. I love that when I was with Janet Jackson, big movies and all that, I'd be up at the dirtiest house party in the hood. People could not believe it. Being

Poet Nikki Giovanni supported Tupac Shakur's right to tell the truth about inner-city life, as he saw it, with his rap lyrics.

up at the party and someone turning around and go[ing], "Oh My God, that's Tupac." [But] that's what kept my sanity, that's what kept me writing, that's what kept me going.[48]

It can be risky for celebrities like Tupac to go out in public without a bodyguard. Many people are jealous of their wealth and fame and some people in poor neighborhoods might even try to rob them. Tupac kept doing it anyway because he wanted to stay the same kind of person he had always been. Over time, however, Tupac began to realize that his lifestyle had changed so dramatically that it was hard to relate to average people and maybe even dangerous. Tupac now lived in luxury condominiums or big houses on the beach in Malibu, California; he drove fancy cars and draped himself in jewels. He realized that his money could make him a target for some poor blacks. He noted, "I grew up around black people, poor people. But I can't live around poor people now cuz they'll rob me. And why would they rob me? Because they're starvin'."[49] Although Tupac's wealth and fame began to separate him from poor blacks, he never lost his passion for exposing the harsh reality of the lives they led.

The Truth About Ghetto Life

African American poet Nikki Giovanni believes that the most important thing Tupac did was to expose the brutal truths of inner-city life. She argues that many people criticized Tupac because they did not want to hear the truth and that they labeled his work "gangsta rap" so no one would take his message seriously. She writes, "So they found a name, Gangsta Rap, to somehow distinguish it from, what? Polite, nice, highly compromised rap? They tried to isolate that beautiful boy who was trying to bring on the truth so that they could flood us [blacks] with lies and excuses [about the way things really were]."[50]

Chapter 4

The "Thug Life" of Tupac Shakur

Tupac Shakur had two sides to his personality, one good and one bad. He admitted once that those conflicting parts of his nature were often at war with each other. "Different things at different times. My own heart sometimes," Tupac admitted. "There's two niggas inside me. One wants to live in peace, and the other won't die unless he's free."[51] This inner conflict was most evident in his rap songs. Some songs stressed the necessity for blacks to fight poverty, racism, and other social factors that made life hard for them. Yet Tupac also glorified many of the ill effects these factors caused, including alcohol and drug abuse, sexual promiscuity, and gang activity. Tupac once tried to explain why his thinking was so divided: "Half of where I came from is the African Independence Movement. Self-defense by any means necessary. The [Black] Panthers element. That came from my family. But my thug half comes from the street element. My reality was the gutter and the street. So I had to follow those rules, too."[52]

The part of Tupac shaped by the "gutter and the street" was also evident in how he conducted his life. Even though Tupac hated drugs because they had almost destroyed his mother, he was addicted to marijuana. It was this part of his personality that made him do senseless, dangerous things that kept getting him into trouble.

"I Had No Record All My Life"

Tupac's first brush with the law came on October 17, 1991, when he was arrested for jaywalking in Oakland, California. Two white officers used a choke hold to subdue him, threw him to the ground, and rammed his head into the sidewalk. The incident happened just a few weeks before *2Pacalypse Now* was released. The timing of the arrest and the debut of his first album provided an ironic bit of reality mirroring art because his songs often featured police brutality:

> I had no record all my life, OK? No record! No police record until I made a record. As my video [from the album] was debuting on MTV, I was behind bars getting beat up by the police department. I was still an N-I-Double-G-A [to white policemen] and they proved it. All this is scars I go to my grave with. All this is learn-to-be-a-nigga scars.[53]

Tupac cooperated with the police officers when they asked for identification. However, he admitted swearing at them later because he thought they were harassing him because he was black. His profanity triggered the beating. After news stories over Tupac's arrest made Oakland police look bad, officials dropped the jaywalking charge. Tupac filed a lawsuit accusing the officers of false arrest and violating his civil rights and he won $42,000 in damages. The incident made Tupac a hero to African Americans. He had stood up to the racist treatment many of them had endured from police and had even embarrassed the police department by winning his lawsuit.

Tupac's first arrest was for a minor offense. But he was soon being accused of much more serious crimes.

Guns and Fistfights

Tupac had never been violent while growing up. Jada Pinkett Smith remembers that he was "always telling me to calm down and stay on the straight and narrow."[54] But success as a rapper changed him. Tupac became more arrogant and aggressive in reacting to other people when they angered him. He began

carrying a gun, partly because a rich celebrity needed protection and partly to live up to his new "gangsta" image. Tupac now had a "crew," a group of friends and associates, including several bodyguards, who accompanied him everywhere.

Russell Simmons, a pioneer in producing rap records, believes the changes in Tupac's lifestyle mirrored those of other entertainers who had became rich and famous. Said Simmons: "Tupac wasn't headed for this [legal problems and violence] any more than, say, [actor] Sean Penn or [singer] Kurt Cobain. It was just that rebelliousness for the sake of it, that wild Rock-n-roll side of him, that did this. The attitude in our world, especially in youth culture, promotes all of this."[55]

According to rap producer Russell Simmons, Tupac Shakur's behavior after becoming rich and famous was no different than any other entertainer who achieved so much at such a young age.

Tupac's new lifestyle exploded into violence on August 22, 1992, when he performed at an outdoor concert in Marin City. When young blacks who had known Tupac when he was poor began taunting him, a fight broke out between them and Tupac's crew. A gun was fired and six-year-old Qa'id Walker-Teal, who was riding a bike nearby, was shot in the head and died. James Cook, a Marin City resident, claimed Tupac's behavior incited the incident. "He was trying to be a gangsta like in the film. He let everyone know he was packing a gat (pistol)," said Cook.[56] The boy's family filed a lawsuit against Tupac.

Interscope Records, his record company, settled it out of court for a reported $300,000 to $500,000, even though Tupac was never directly linked to the shooting.

Another incident occurred in March 1993. Tupac and some friends were accused of beating up a limousine driver who drove them to the Fox studio in Hollywood, California, to tape an episode of *In Living Color*. The fight began when the driver accused Tupac's friends of using drugs. Tupac was arrested for assault but the charges were dropped. The volatile rapper was not so lucky a few months later when he attacked movie directors Albert and Allen Hughes. He was angry at the brothers because they had dropped him from the cast of *Menace II Society*. When Tupac accidentally ran into the brothers at the taping of a video, he attacked them. Tupac hit Allen but Albert ran off before he could rough him up. Tupac was sentenced to fifteen days in jail for the incident.

Tupac Shakur's temper often got the better of him, as in the time he was sentenced to fifteen days in jail for assaulting Albert and Allen Hughes, pictured.

The sentence was not his first. A year earlier Tupac had been jailed for an incident at one of his concerts.

His Rowdy Concerts

The out-of-control behavior that was becoming part of Tupac's personal life was spilling over into his concerts. During a show in Lansing, Michigan, on April 5, 1993, Tupac was arrested for swinging a baseball bat at a local rapper who he thought was going to attack him. "I took a swing that backed him up," Tupac said.[57] Convicted of misdemeanor assault and battery, Tupac received a ten-day jail sentence for threatening the rapper.

At a concert in Milwaukee on September 3, 1994, one of his bodyguards reportedly displayed a gun on stage after the audience began shouting at Tupac and throwing trash on the stage. When Tupac reportedly said, "Some people might not leave here tonight because they might be dead,"[58] rap fans fled the Milwaukee Arena. Police later found two guns in Tupac's dressing room. He was not arrested but his act was dropped from the tour of several rap stars called the Phat Rap Phest Tour. There was a violent postscript to his appearance. Four days later two eighteen-year-old Milwaukee youths—Curtis Walker and Denziss Jackson—shot to death police officer William Robertson. They claimed that listening to "Soulja's Story" incited them to kill Robertson.

Tupac also began showing a disdain for the law in his concerts. On October 31, 1993, he performed at Clark University in Atlanta, Georgia. He had been warned that he would be arrested if his show involved any drug use, but during his performance he held up a marijuana cigarette and asked spectators, "What I want to know is, if I light this, will you let them take me to jail?"[59] The crowd cheered but Tupac did not light the cigarette.

At that time Tupac was living in Atlanta. While driving home that night, he and some friends saw two white men harassing a black motorist on the side of a road. Tupac stopped to help the motorist and began arguing with the two men. Shots were exchanged and both white men received minor wounds. The men were Mark and Scott Whitwell, brothers and off-duty Atlanta police officers. Tupac was charged with aggravated assault, but the charges were dropped because the brothers were drunk, armed with guns stolen from a police evidence locker, and lied to their superiors about the incident.

Once again, Tupac had escaped serious legal trouble. His luck with the law would run out two weeks later.

Tupac Goes to Prison

Tupac liked to party at expensive nightclubs. On November 14, Tupac and some friends were drinking and dancing at Nells in New York City when he met twenty-year-old Ayanna Jackson. She accompanied Tupac back to the Le Parker Meridien Hotel, where he and his entourage were staying. Tupac and Jackson had sex and she then left.

Tupac Shakur was arrested in November 1993 on charges of sexual assault and possession of weapons.

Jackson returned to his hotel suite four days later. Tupac said she gave him a massage and he then left her in a room with some friends because he wanted to get some sleep. He woke up to hear Jackson screaming, "'Rape! Rape!' [That] I raped her. She's yellin' at me, 'This isn't the last you're going to see of me' [and] the next thing I know I'm going to jail."[60] Tupac and three friends were arrested for sexually assaulting Jackson. Despite his claim that he did not have sex with her that day, Tupac was charged with sodomy, sexual abuse, and possession of weapons after two guns were found in his suite.

Tupac's career suffered during the months of legal battles that followed. His violent image led director John Singleton to drop him from the movie *Higher Learning*, and he had to cancel concerts to make court appearances. In November 1994 Tupac was

Tupac's Tattoos

Like many young people, Tupac decorated his body with tattoos. The tattoos that covered his chest, stomach, back, and arms were not simply body art but statements about his political and personal philosophy. His most famous tattoo was THUG LIFE, which arced across his muscled abdomen; the letters were outlined, the "I" replaced by the drawing of a bullet. Just above that tattoo was the phrase "50 Niggaz"; it represented blacks in all fifty states and incorporated an AK-47 rifle into its design. A panther head that adorned his upper left arm honored his family's association with the Black Panther party. A figure of Jesus on a burning cross wearing a crown of thorns lay below the panther with the phrase "Only God Can Judge Me." The tattoo honored God and was also a defiant declaration that Tupac did not think anyone else had a right to judge him. On his back Tupac had a cross and "Exodus 18:11," the Bible verse that reads, "Now I know that the Lord is greater than all gods." Other tattoos included Tupac's nicknames "Makaveli" and "2PAC."

back in New York for his trial. After a long day in court, he went to a record studio to perform on a rap song for a friend. He entered the studio's lobby shortly after midnight on November 29 and was waiting for an elevator when two men robbed him. They took $40,000 in jewelry and shot him five times; bullets struck Tupac in the groin, torso, and arm and grazed his scalp. Tupac later said he remembered little of being shot:

> [When] I got to Bellevue Hospital, the doctor was going, "Oh my God!" I was, like, "What? what?" [The doctor] said, "You don't know how lucky you are. You got shot five times." It was, like, weird. I did not want to believe it. I could only remember that first shot, then everything went blank.[61]

About fifty family members, including his mother, sister, and aunt, rushed to the hospital. Although he needed surgery, Tupac, miraculously, was not seriously injured. The next day he left the hospital despite the protests of doctors who said he needed more care.

In a show of toughness, Tupac returned to the courtroom on December 1. The jury that day issued a verdict that cleared him of sodomy and weapons charges but found him guilty of sexual abuse. On February 14, 1995, Tupac was sentenced to one-and-a-half to four-and-a-half years in prison.

A Caged Rapper

Tupac was sent to Rikers Island, a prison in New York City, and two months later was transferred to the Clinton Correctional Facility in upstate New York. Always rebellious, Tupac could not refrain from mouthing off to racist white guards who called black prisoners "niggers" and taunted him in other ways. He explained, "For the first half of my stay there, me and the guards had problems. I got smacked, treated bad . . . they just did everything they could to try and break me. As soon as I got there they went, 'There's the rich nigger.'"[62]

Some prisoners also resented Tupac because of his fame and riches, but for the most part he was treated with respect as a celebrity and a tough individual. He even became friendly with a skinhead, a young white racist, and they spent a lot of time talking. "It blew my mind," Tupac said, "that we could be two totally different people, with such totally different views and really talk and hear each other."[63] Tupac even signed autographs for the prisoner's relatives.

In prison Tupac suffered from withdrawal from marijuana, the drug he was addicted to. "I had to go through what life is like when you've been smoking weed for as long as I have and then you stop," he said. Without marijuana, his emotions were confused and he had trouble functioning. Life became easier, however, as the drug cleared out of his body: "Then every day I started doing, like, a thousand push-ups for myself. I was reading whole books in one day, and writing, and that was putting me in a peace of mind."[64]

Beginning in February 1993 Tupac Shakur spent two months at Rikers Island prison in New York City, but was transferred to another facility in upstate New York for the next six months of his sentence.

Topping the Charts in Prison

Tupac was delighted when "Me Against the World" became the number one album while he was still in prison:

For the brief moment my record got released, I was the number one record. People made me number one. And I loved them for that. It was a trip, it was a trip every time they [prison guards] used to say something bad to me, I'd be like, "That's alright, I got the number one record in the country." Cuz they used to tell me stuff like "You're in jail, won't be any more rapping for a long time for you, huh? Ha, ha, ha." I'd be like, "Well, actually, my album is number one in the country right now. I just beat Bruce Springsteen." And they used to be like, "Go back to your cell." . . . To me, it'll always be my favorite album.

Jacob Hoye and Karolyn Ali, eds., *Tupac: Resurrection 1971–1996*. New York: Atria, 2003, p. 166.

Tupac was lonely despite visits from friends and relatives. That was why he married girlfriend Keisha Morris on April 29, 1995, in a ceremony at the Clinton prison. "I married her because I was in jail. I was alone. I didn't want to be alone,"[65] he admitted. Although the marriage was annulled a few months later, the two remained good friends.

Tupac Gets Out of Prison

Tupac served only eight months in prison. His lawyers appealed the guilty verdict immediately after the trial on the grounds that Tupac had not personally abused Jackson. In October 1995 they won the right to appeal his conviction. The ruling meant that Tupac could be freed if he could post $1.4 million bail. Tupac could not raise the bail, but Marion "Suge" Knight, the head of

Tupac Reflects on Being a Celebrity

Like many celebrities, Tupac thought that the news media made his life more difficult by publicizing his legal and personal problems so the whole world knew about them. Tupac commented on this problem in an interview on April 19, 1996, on California radio station KMEL:

> I can't really take [his problems with the law] personal because I'm a reflection of the community. All young Black males are going through [problems like he had]. To me it's not personal because they're all going through it. The only thing that makes it different and original with me is that people get to watch it from beginning to end like it's a soap opera. You get to watch [his legal and personal problems] and with everyone else they get to hide and go to their homes and get over it. With me you see me dealing with my greatest pains.

"Tupac Shakur Speaks." Interviews on a CD accompanying the book *Tupac Shakur Legacy* by Jamal Joseph. New York: Atria, 2006.

Death Row Records, came to his rescue. Aware that Tupac was still wildly popular, Knight helped Tupac post his bail as part of a contract Tupac signed to make three albums for Knight's company. In April 1995 Tupac's third album, *Me Against the World*, had debuted in first place on *Billboard*'s pop chart. He was the first person ever to have a number one record while in prison.

Tupac was freed on October 13. He immediately flew to California to begin creating some of his most successful songs.

Chapter 5

The Mysterious Murder of Tupac Shakur

Six days after his release from prison on October 13, 1995, Tupac Shakur talked to a newspaper reporter in Los Angeles. Tupac was happy to be free again and said he was already recording for Death Row Records. When asked about his many problems with the law in the last few years, Tupac admitted that he had "made some mistakes" but denied that he was the violent lawbreaker many people believed him to be:

> Let me say for the record, I am not a gangster and never have been. I'm not the thief who grabs your purse. I'm not the guy who jacks your car. I'm not down with people who steal and hurt others. I'm just a brother who fights back. I'm not some violent closet psycho. I've got a job. I'm an artist.[66]

Tupac's job was creating rap records, and he was doing it at a phenomenal pace. Working nearly around the clock after getting out of prison, Tupac had already churned out fourteen songs by the time he talked with the reporter. He was recording *All Eyez on Me*, the album he would release in February 1996 as rap's first double CD. Today, it is considered one of the finest rap albums ever made.

In his interview, however, Tupac was more concerned with healing his tarnished image than promoting his work. He wanted the world to know that despite his past problems, he was now a different person.

A New Tupac

Some people change while they are in prison. Being locked up with nothing to do gives inmates time to reflect on their lives and what they did wrong to wind up in prison. Prisoners who were addicted to drugs and alcohol, as Tupac had been, can think clearly about their past because they are no longer intoxicated. In an interview he gave while in prison, Tupac explained that he had

When Tupac started his new life after prison, he surrounded himself with family, including his sister Sekyiwa, pictured, and friends he had made before he became famous.

Tupac's Big Mouth

Tupac realized that part of his problem was his lack of fear in saying anything that was on his mind. When asked once what he was best known for, he replied,

> My big mouth. My big mouth. I got a big mouth. I can't help it, I talk from my heart, I'm real. You know what I'm sayin'? What ever comes, comes. But it's not my fault. I'm trying to find my way in the world. I'm trying to be somebody instead of making money off everybody, you know what I'm sayin'? So I go down paths that haven't been traveled before. And I usually mess up, but I learn. I come back stronger. I'm not talkin' ignorant. So obviously I put thought into what I do. So I think my mouth and my controversy. I haven't been out of the paper since I joined Digital Underground. And that's good for me cuz I don't want to be forgotten. If I'm forgotten then that means I'm comfortable and that means I think everything is OK.

Armond White, *Rebel for the Hell of It: The Life of Tupac Shakur*. New York: Thunder's Mouth, 1997, p. 175.

already realized how foolish he had been acting and that he wanted to become a better person: "The [marijuana] addict in Tupac is dead. The excuse maker in Tupac is dead. The vengeful Tupac is dead. The Tupac that would stand by and let dishonorable things happen is dead. God let me live for me to do something extremely extraordinary, and that's what I have to do."[67]

Tupac still claimed that he had never sexually abused Ayanna Jackson, but he admitted that he shared responsibility for what happened that night. "That was my fault," he said, "that I had that kind of environment around me."[68] By "environment," Tupac meant the members of his crew who assaulted Jackson. After he was released from prison, Tupac changed the people he surrounded himself with. He reunited with family members and longtime friends because he no longer trusted his crew. "I don't have friends," he said. "I have family. You're either my all-the-way family or just somebody on the outside."[69]

His mother had stopped using drugs several years earlier. Tupac moved Afeni, his aunt, and other relatives from New York to California. They lived near him in apartments or houses he paid for and sometimes with him in his large house on the coast in Malibu. He enjoyed spending time with his sister Sekyiwa and his many young nieces, nephews, and cousins. For his personal staff, he hired friends he had known since before he became famous, including Molly Monjauze, a high school classmate from Baltimore.

The rapper did not spend as much time with his family and friends as he would have liked, however, because he was working so hard on his career.

Making Records and Movies

The creative burst of energy Tupac enjoyed when he was released from prison lasted until his murder less than a year later. Long hours of writing lyrics and recording songs resulted in rap's first double CD as well as a backlog of more than two hundred songs that would be released after his death. His hard work was motivated by a desire to succeed and his hatred of East Coast rappers like Puffy Combs and Biggie Smalls (also known as the Notorious B.I.G.), a former friend with whom he had recorded songs.

A rivalry had always existed between East and West Coast rappers over who was the best. This rivalry had been bitter at times. It became ugly after Tupac went to prison because he believed eastern rappers tried then to tarnish his image and ruin him by making disrespectful comments about his situation. He became so angry at the attacks that he gave up plans to end his career when he got out of prison. He explained, "I was really going to quit rapping. All I wanted to do was get out the game, end everything and walk away from it. I try to get out the game and they want to dirty up my memory, they want to dirty up everything I worked for. So instead of quitting they made me come back more relentless."[70]

East Coast rappers Lil' Kim, Notorious B.I.G., and Sean Puffy Combs in 1995 at the Billboard Music Awards.

Tupac also believed that East Coast rappers had arranged the near-fatal robbery in 1994. Combs and Smalls had been with him when he was shot. In a prison interview, Tupac said that, afterward, "Nobody [who witnessed it] approached me. I noticed that nobody would look at me." He believed that the way the other rappers acted was a sign of guilt. He also said he had heard rumors that connected them to the robbery. Tupac attacked them for their involvement in two songs in *All Eyez on Me*. In "2 of Amerikaz Most Wanted," Tupac hints that Combs and Smalls were behind the robbery. In "Hit 'Em Up," Tupac vows vengeance against whoever staged the robbery: "Who shot me? But ya punks didn't finish, Now you're about to feel the wrath of a menace."[71] Tupac also boasted in that song of having sex with Faith Evans, Biggie's estranged wife.

Tupac and costar Tim Roth in a scene from Gridlock'd.

Tupac was also busy making movies. In *Gridlock'd*, he played an addict trying to quit using drugs. He got good reviews, which he admitted he needed to clean up his image. "It was real important for me to do well," Tupac said, "in terms of letting people understand that I was professional. That I wasn't the demonized monster the press made me out to be."[72] In his next movie, *Gang Related*, he played a crooked cop. The filming finished one week before he was shot and killed in Las Vegas.

The Murder of Tupac Shakur

Tupac knew heavyweight champion Mike Tyson. He even felt a kinship with him because Tyson also claimed he had been wrongfully convicted of sexual assault. Tupac went to Las Vegas to root for Tyson in his fight against Bruce Seldon at the MGM Grand Hotel on the night of September 7, 1996. Suge Knight and Tupac's fiancée, Kidada Jones, the daughter of famed musician Quincy Jones, went with him.

Tyson knocked out Seldon two minutes into the title bout, which therefore ended unexpectedly early, before 9 P.M. On leaving the hotel, Tupac encountered Orlando Anderson, a member of the Crips, a Los Angeles gang. Tupac began fighting with Anderson because he recognized him as the person who had stolen a medallion from an acquaintance a few months earlier. Tupac, Knight, and several members of Knight's entourage kicked and stomped Anderson in a brutal beating caught on hotel security videotapes.

Tupac and the others then left the hotel, just before 9 P.M., and made stops at Tupac's hotel and Knight's house. They left there about 11:10 P.M. in a ten-car motorcade headed for a

A few hours before he was shot, Tupac Shakur attended a boxing match at the MGM Grand Hotel in Las Vegas.

nightclub. Tupac was riding with Knight in his black BMW 750 on Flamingo Road when a white Cadillac pulled up next to their car, which had stopped at a red light. Two men got out of the Cadillac and from less than ten feet away fired thirteen rounds into the BMW. Tupac was hit four times—twice in the chest, the wounds that would kill him—while Knight suffered a minor head injury.

Tupac was taken by ambulance to the University of Nevada Medical Center for surgery, which included removal of his right lung. As he was being loaded into the ambulance, Frank Alexander, one of Knight's entourage, heard Tupac say softly, "I'm a dying man."[73]

The Aftermath of the Shooting

Friends and relatives flew to Las Vegas to be with Tupac. A huge crowd of fans gathered outside the hospital, waiting anxiously to learn if the rapper they loved would survive. Tupac remained in critical condition for six days. He died of respiratory failure and cardiopulmonary arrest at 4:03 P.M. on September 13.

No one mourned his death more than Afeni Shakur, who had feared for his life since the day he was born because of her Black Panther background and the poverty and violence that surrounded them. "It's funny," she said, "because I never believed he would live. Every five years, I'd be just amazed that he made it to five, he made it to ten, he made it to fifteen."[74] Afeni quickly had her son's body cremated at the nearby Davis Mortuary. She and other relatives left Las Vegas the next day. Several memorial services were held around the nation in cities like New York and Atlanta. In Malibu, family and close friends had a private ceremony.

Police meanwhile were trying to find Tupac's killer. In the immediate aftermath of the fatal shooting, they were able to discover very little about what had happened. The day after the shooting, Sergeant Kevin Manning of the Las Vegas metropolitan police department's homicide unit said, "The only evidence we have is the number of rounds fired and the physical evidence."[75] The investigation into Tupac's death was hampered by a lack of cooperation from Knight and other people in his entourage, who claimed they had not seen the shooting because they were looking elsewhere. Police spokesman Phil Roland admitted, "We're puzzled that [Knight's] whole entourage had their heads turned and didn't see anything."[76] However, one person gave a brief description of the shooting to a reporter. According to this witness, identified only as a member of Knight's entourage, "Two men got out of the [Cadillac] because the traffic was stalled. Then they just started spraying bullets. I could see Tupac trying to jump into the back seat. That's how his chest got exposed so much."[77]

Police were able to accumulate few facts about Tupac's death. However, they developed several theories about why he was killed.

Kidada Jones was engaged to Tupac Shakur at the time of his death.

Six days after being shot while riding in Suge Knight's car, Tupac Shakur died from his injuries.

Gangs, Knight, or His Own Lifestyle?

Las Vegas police claimed that Tupac's shooting was gang-related. Sergeant Chuck Cassell of the police department's gang unit said that Tupac was probably the victim of a battle between two gangs, the Bloods and the Crips. Las Vegas had five thousand gang members, and they often attacked each other. Cassell believed gangs were involved because Tupac fit the image of a gang member and because of the earlier beating incident involving Anderson, a Crip. Cassell said, "Look at [Tupac's] tattoos and album covers—that's not the Jackson Five. [The Jackson Five were a popular black group whose members had an image that was clean-cut compared to rappers like Tupac.] [It] looks like a case of live by the sword, die by the sword."[78]

Some people suspected that Knight had ordered Tupac's shooting because he feared Tupac was going to leave the record company. However, many people had trouble believing that because Knight could have been killed in the hail of bullets that took Tupac's life. In August Tupac had fired David Kenner as his attorney. Kenner also represented Death Row, and the firing was seen as Tupac's first step in severing his ties with Knight. Tupac was grateful to Knight for helping him get out of jail, but he had begun to suspect that Knight was cheating him out of record profits. Knight also had a dark reputation for reportedly using violent tactics to make rappers sign with him or do what he wanted. For example, he allegedly coerced Vanilla Ice into signing over royalties from his album *To the Extreme* by dangling the rapper by his ankles over a hotel balcony and threatening to drop him.

However, there is no hard evidence to support the theory that either Knight or gangs were involved in Tupac's death. The simplest and most believable explanation is that Tupac was the victim of the lifestyle he led, one that had long put him in contact

Did Tupac Shakur Predict His Death?

When Tupac was killed by gunfire in Las Vegas in September 1996, many people believed he had a premonition of an early death because of statements he had made or things he had done. Of all those ill omens of death, none was more dramatic than the video for "I Ain't Mad at Cha," which was released shortly after Tupac was murdered. In the song and video, the character Tupac is singing about is shot and killed while walking down a street. When he arrives in heaven, it is populated by great black entertainers of the past. He is greeted at the gates of heaven by someone resembling comedian Redd Foxx. They are soon joined by legendary singers and musicians such as Louis Armstrong, Josephine Baker, Miles Davis, Marvin Gaye, Jimi Hendrix, and Billie Holiday. Afeni Shakur once said she believed that the song was her son's way of making peace with God.

with many violent people in a variety of social situations. Tupac had made enemies by his behavior and there were reports that death threats had been made against him. Realizing his potential danger, he had begun to wear a bullet-proof vest, although he was not wearing it the night he was fatally wounded. Dana Smith, a friend from Tupac's school days in Baltimore, said the type of violence that killed Tupac was inevitable if he was going to live the life he wanted, mingling with his fans whenever he could. Smith said, "Tupac could try to stay out of trouble, stay in the hotel, but that's not real. If he did that, people would call him snobby. You can't get away from the street. That's where you're from. You've got to give that love back."[79]

Some people speculate that Marion "Suge" Knight, right, was involved in Tupac Shakur's murder, but no hard evidence can prove this theory.

Tupac Shakur's Charitable Works

Tupac became involved in community and charitable programs when he got out of prison. A Place Called Home in Los Angeles is an agency that helps youths by providing counseling, recreation, and health services. Tupac helped organize a concert to raise funds for the program and solicited donations from his friends. In an interview on April 19, 1996, on radio station KMEL, Tupac talked of other community projects:

> I'm starting to put out some calendars for charity. I'm gonna start a little youth league in California. I wanna have like a Pop Warner League except the rappers fund it and they're the head coaches. Have a league where you can get a big trophy with diamonds in it for a [young black] to stay drug free and stay in school. That's the only way you can be on the team. We'll have fun and eat pizza and have the finest girls there and throw concerts at the end of the year. That's what I mean by giving back.

"Tupac Shakur Speaks." Interviews on a CD accompanying the book *Tupac Shakur Legacy* by Jamal Joseph. New York: Atria, 2006.

"Rules of the Game"

This last theory about Tupac's death is the simplest and easiest to believe. Tupac himself understood that people who are close to violence often die violent deaths. This is how Tupac responded once when asked to explain the shooting death of a friend: "Ain't no words. The rules of the game are so self-explanatory. What goes 'round comes 'round."[80] Many people believed the saying applied to his death as well and that Tupac, like many other young black men, died because he made so many wrong choices while living the "thug life" he glorified. However, no one really knows to this day who was responsible for killing him.

Chapter 6

Tupac Shakur: The Immortal Rapper

When Tupac Shakur was a teenager in Baltimore, his mother took him to a Salvation Army store, one of the few places where the poor family could afford to shop. Afeni Shakur bought him a record player and an album by folk singer Don McLean. Tupac listened to the record over and over again, including the song "American Pie," a classic about the deaths on February 3, 1959, of rock-and-roll legends Buddy Holly, Richie Valens, and J.P. Richardson ("The Big Bopper"). The song claims that when their airplane crashed, a musical era ended and it was thus "the day the music died."[81] But when Tupac was murdered in Las Vegas, his music did not die with him. Tupac's sensational death merely marked the beginning of a new phase of his career that would make the rapper more revered and famous than he had been while alive.

From 1991 until 1995, Tupac had produced five solo albums that sold more than 20 million copies. In the decade after his death in 1996, a dozen albums featuring his voice and songs were released and sold an additional 53 million copies. Tupac's film career also continued. Two movies Tupac finished before his murder—*Gridlock'd* and *Gang Related*—debuted in 1997. More amazingly, in 2003 his voice and image starred in *Tupac: Resurrection*, a documentary about his life. The movie featured extensive film clips of Tupac, and the dead rapper served as the film's narrator through audio excerpts from past interviews. In addition, two books of his poetry were published—*The Rose That Grew from Concrete* (1999) and *Inside a Thug's Heart* (2004).

Michael Eric Dyson, author of *Holler If You Hear Me: Searching for Tupac Shakur*, claims that the tremendous output of Tupac's work after his death has ensured that his "lyrical and literary

The rocky relationship between Tupac Shakur and his mother Afeni is chronicled in the 2003 documentary **Tupac: Resurrection.**

immortality is secure."[82] But Tupac also lives on in other ways. Makaveli is a brand of clothing named after one of Tupac's rap nicknames, and the Tupac Amaru Shakur Foundation helps young people develop the type of creative talents that made Tupac successful. Tupac also exists in cyberspace through a host of Web sites, including 2paclegacy.com, his official site—a Google search of "Tupac" turns up more than 8.5 million hits.

Tupac owes much of his enduring immortality to the single-minded drive of one person: his mother, Afeni Shakur.

"My Duties Did Not End"

Tupac loved Afeni Shakur even when they were estranged by her drug use. After Afeni quit drugs and alcohol on May 12, 1991, Tupac joyfully reunited with her. He liked to boast, "When my mother got clean we got real close again. My mom is the bomb, you know? World's best mom."[83] Afeni was shattered when her beloved son died. She quickly channeled her grief and bitterness over his loss into a quest to keep his memory alive and to show the world that her son was more than a "gangsta rapper" who had fallen victim to the senseless violence he often sang about. Said Afeni: "When I lost my son, I had to remember I have a responsibility to my son to stay clean [from drugs] and live up to my duties. And my duties did not end when Tupac died."[84]

Afeni's first battle to rescue her son's legacy was to confront Suge Knight, the Death Row recording executive she believed had been robbing Tupac of millions of dollars. When Tupac died, he had less than $100,000 in his bank account and did not own the car he was driving. Afeni and lawyers she hired discovered that Death Row had been cheating Tupac out of royalties and using accounting tricks to steal his money. She sued Knight to get the stolen funds back and to gain control of master tapes of nearly two hundred unreleased songs Tupac had recorded. She wanted control so she could release his work in a positive way that would polish his artistic image. She feared Death Row would flood the market with cheap new Tupac albums just to make money.

Where Lies Tupac?

After Tupac's body was cremated, friends and family members scattered his ashes in several places. In *Tupac Shakur Legacy*, author Jamal Joseph states that "the unique distribution of his ashes signified all the lives he'd touched as well as the many lives he himself had lived." The biography, which was written with the cooperation of Tupac's family, says that some of his ashes were placed on a farm in Lumberton, North Carolina; in Atlanta; in Harlem; and in the sea off Malibu. Joseph also claims that some friends mixed Tupac's ashes with marijuana and smoked them at a memorial service. In 2006 Afeni Shakur announced she was going to travel to South Africa on the tenth anniversary of Tupac's death and bury his ashes there in honor of the struggle waged by black South Africans to end apartheid. Although her trip was called off in September 2006, she said she would go at a later date. The incident raised questions about how many places have become a resting spot for at least a tiny part of the slain rapper's body.

Jamal Joseph, *Tupac Shakur Legacy*. New York: Atria, 2006, p. 60.

A vicious legal battle ensued between Afeni and Interscope, the firm that owned Death Row. She eventually won control of the songs but agreed to pay Interscope a percentage of future income from their sale. Afeni said she had the will and strength to fight for her son because of her revolutionary past: "Had it not been for my life as a woman in the Black Panther Party, I wouldn't have been able to save my son's music. Had it not been for membership in the Black Panther Party, I wouldn't have been able to tell Suge Knight 'no.'"[85]

Afeni named the company she created to produce Tupac's records Amaru, which was his middle name. But the first record released after Tupac died came out before his mother ever won her legal battle.

The Best-Selling Rapper Ever

On November 5, 1996, less than two months after Tupac died, Death Row released the last album Tupac had made during his life. It was called *The Don Killuminati: The 7 Day Theory*. Tupac had adopted the alias "Makaveli" in this album because he had been impressed with books he read in prison by Niccolò Machiavelli, a sixteenth-century Italian philosopher. The

Snoop Dogg, left, pictured here with Tupac Shakur at the 1996 MTV Music Awards, collaborated with Tupac on many rap projects.

album's dramatic cover depicted Tupac nailed to a cross under a crown of thorns; a map of the country's major gang areas was superimposed on his face.

Fans bought 664,000 copies of the album in one week and in the next decade they purchased almost 2 million more copies. Amaru Records has released eleven posthumous albums since then, including *Pac's Life*, which came out on November 21, 2006. Like his other posthumous albums, *Pac's Life* contained previously unreleased material by Tupac as well as guest appearances by rappers like Ludacris, Snoop Dogg, Keyshia Cole, and Ashanti. By the time *Pac's Life* was released, sales of Tupac's albums had topped 73 million to make him the best-selling rapper ever.

Many people have been astounded at the seemingly limitless flow of material from someone who has been dead since 1996. According to Afeni, however, it was easy to create so many albums because "Tupac left us the blueprints to follow."[86] When Tupac died, he left behind not only recordings but detailed notes on how he wanted the songs presented. In 2006 Afeni promised that the company would release even more songs because "our purpose is to make sure everything Tupac wrote will see the light of day."[87] The posthumous albums have sold well—four of them have hit No. 1 in sales—and even his older songs are still popular. A poll that *Rolling Stone* magazine conducted in 2006 showed that U.S. soldiers in Iraq ranked the 1996 tune "Hit 'Em Up" fourth on a list of their top ten songs.

Afeni's quest to produce all of Tupac's songs is just one part of her mission to make sure the world never forgets her son. Another major effort in her crusade was to produce a documentary film of his life.

Afeni Resurrects Tupac

Tupac: Resurrection opened in theaters across the nation in 2003. For his fans, it was eerie but thrilling to hear Tupac narrate his own life through skillful editing of his interviews. The commentary Tupac provided for the film gave a powerful veracity to the story of his life as it unfolded on the screen. Afeni said she wanted the movie to correct wrong impressions the public had about Tupac:

> The past seven years have been extremely painful, watching and listening while others incorrectly attempted to define who my son really was [through books and articles]. Now, through patience, the strength of my family and faith in God, the true story of Tupac is finally being shared with the world, through his own words, music and images. Understanding who Tupac really was can only enhance his legacy.[88]

The movie was well received but some critics believed it downplayed Tupac's negative side to make him seem like a better person than he was. Tupac's mother also coordinated publication of a companion book to the movie with the same title. It had pictures, poems, lyrics from his songs, and quotes from Tupac, but no narrative to explain his life.

Many people have accused Afeni of trying to clean up Tupac's image with projects like these. She does not care what other people think. Asked about the violence, obscene language, and negative images that filled many of Tupac's songs, she responded:

> I am proud of everything my son has done as an artist. It's not like I agreed with everything he ever said. But I think you should judge an artist by his body of work. In the 1950s, they said worse things about rock'n'roll, they said worse things about the blues [than about rap]. Music makes its own evolution. In ten years hip-hop will still be here but we'll be condemning another music.[89]

His mother is not the only person who has judged Tupac on his work's overall merit rather than the negative images and words in his songs that have offended some people. For those who are willing to consider his entire career, Tupac is not only a great rapper but a great artist.

"A Ghetto Dickens"

Tupac believed that the media had always unfairly judged him by concentrating on the sensational parts of his life and songs.

Shortly after he was released from prison in 1995, he claimed that this type of media coverage had given the general public a false image of who he was: "The thing that bothers me is that it seems like all the sensitive stuff I write just goes unnoticed. The media doesn't get who I am at all. Or maybe it [his sensitive side] doesn't fit into those negative stories they like to write."[90]

Students can enroll in dance, vocal, and other fine arts classes at the Tupac Amaru Shakur Center for the Arts in Stone Mountain, Georgia.

The Unsolved Murder of Tupac Shakur

A decade after Tupac Shakur was shot and killed in Las Vegas, his murder was still unsolved. The investigation that followed Tupac's death never uncovered any solid leads about his killer. The strongest suspect was Orlando Anderson, the gang member Tupac helped beat up the night he was killed. Police suspected that Anderson or his gang, the Crips, attacked Tupac for revenge. Officials, however, never had enough evidence to charge Anderson, who was shot to death in Compton, California, on May 29, 1998. Afeni Shakur has criticized police for failing to find her son's killer. In a *Time* magazine story in 2006 on the tenth anniversary of Tupac's death, Afeni said she had little hope the case would ever be solved:

> "They still haven't solved Malcolm's murder. They still haven't solved Martin's murder," Shakur says, alluding to the suspicions around the deaths of Malcolm X and Martin Luther King Jr. In a flash, the fire of her Panther past rears up. "When they solve those, then they can get to Tupac."

Quoted in Ta-Nehissi Coates, "A Tale of Two Mothers," *Time*, September 25, 2006, p. 74.

Tupac, however, would have loved much that has been written about him since he died.

According to biographer Michael Eric Dyson, the dramatic, eloquent way in which Tupac criticized the social and economic woes of blacks elevated him to the status of one of literature's greatest novelists—Charles Dickens. Dyson argues that "Tupac's language was inflamed with love for the desperately poor. He was a ghetto Dickens who explained the plight of the downtrodden in rebellious rhyme."[91] Dickens's novels are passionate commentaries on poverty, class, and other social problems in nineteenth-century England. Dyson believes that Tupac brought the same artistry to highlighting problems like police brutality, unwed teenage mothers, and absentee fathers.

Praise for Tupac

Tupac once boasted that college professors and students would one day study him the way they did William Shakespeare, whose plays he loved. Tupac's prophecy has come true. Some colleges offer classes devoted to his music and Harvard University in 2004 hosted a scholarly conference on Tupac sponsored by the Hip-Hop Archive. Wayne State University professor Walter Edwards wrote a scholarly article about Tupac's poetry in *The Rose That Grew from Concrete*. According to Edwards, "The poems in the anthology reveal that at age 19, Tupac was a young man of unusual social intelligence who possessed a gift for communicating his ideas in verse. My sense is that Tupac was on his way to finding his voice as a lyrical poet but chose to interrupt that development in favor of his career as a rap artist."[92] Another college professor who has studied Tupac is Mark Anthony Neal, of the African and African American Studies program at Duke University. Neal believes that what made Tupac great was the dynamic way he performed and even lived:

> Tupac was never the best rapper in terms of flow or lyrics. But what enabled him to transcend everybody else in the room was that he had a sense of performance. When Tupac was on-stage, in the broad sense, he always knew how to live up to the hype of the crowd—even if it was being wheeled out of the hospital the first time he was shot. He had that flair for the dramatic, which speaks to his real talent: as an actor.[93]

Afeni claims that Tupac's artistic talents helped him be successful despite poverty, racism, and other obstacles he encountered in his life. "The arts saved Tupac," she has said.[94] That belief led Afeni to start the Tupac Amaru Shakur Center for the Arts in Stone Mountain, Georgia. The center is devoted to helping young people develop similar talents so they can also be successful.

The center's campus features a statue of Tupac that was dedicated on the ninth anniversary of his death in 2005. Although that statue is a symbol of his death, many of his fans have had trouble believing that Tupac is really dead.

Is Tupac Still Alive?

When beloved entertainers die, many fans refuse to accept the truth because they do not want their idol to be gone. Even though Elvis Presley died on August 16, 1977, some people still believe he is alive. When Tupac died, some of his fans claimed that he had faked his death because he was afraid of going back to prison or wanted to be safe from people he believed were trying to kill him. Some theories even claim that his mother is helping him hide.

The belief that Tupac was still alive bothered Afeni until she talked to a black college student who defended it by saying, "If they have Elvis, why can't we have Tupac?"[95] That comment made Afeni realize that her son's fans wanted to believe the crazy idea because they loved Tupac so much. And that made her feel good that her son would never be forgotten.

Should Tupac Shakur Be a Role Model?

Tupac Shakur never cared what people thought about him. He got a nose stud even though he knew some people would not like it. He had the same attitude about the elaborate tattoos he chose to adorn his body, the lyrics he wrote, and the personal choices he made in his daily life, such as using drugs. Tupac brushed off criticism of his personal and professional life by claiming that he had been shaped by a culture that had many faults: "I was raised in this society, so there's no way you can expect me to be a perfect person. I'm-a do what I'm-a do. That's how I feel. I'll do whatever I like. I'm not a role model."[96]

Even though he refused to accept that status, Tupac was a role model to many young people. Young blacks, especially, envied his success, wealth, and the freedom with which he lived, and they believed they could get the same things for themselves by acting like him. Many people thought that Tupac was someone to admire because he was a basically good person who had accomplished a great deal. However, the idea of Tupac as a role model angered many other people, who believed he had led an immoral life and had more negative than positive qualities. On the subject of Tupac, there was little middle ground—people either hated him or loved him.

Tupac's Detractors

Tupac's critics believed he should not be revered because of his criminal record, his lifestyle, and the content of his songs, which were often lewd and seemed to promote violence and gang activity. In 2002 Michael Medved, a conservative radio talk-show host, attacked Tupac's continuing glorification through books, newspaper articles, Web sites, and the upcoming film *Tupac: Resurrection*. Medved wrote, "The intensifying exploitation of slain rap artist Tupac Shakur highlights the sick, shameless show-business tendency to glorify violent and self-destructive black thugs."[97]

Although Medved was white, as were many of Tupac's critics, Tupac also had black detractors. John McWhorter, a university professor who has written about race relations and black culture, claims Tupac is given too much credit for attacking poverty, racism, and police brutality. He argues that Tupac's ideas were not original because everyone already knew that such social ills were harming blacks. McWhorter also claims that the lessons Tupac taught young blacks were negative: "Alas, this allegedly exemplary voice of black America is teaching almost nothing but hopelessness. Again and again, he recommends rage [as a solution to problems]."[98]

People also criticized Tupac because he had made so many poor choices in his personal life. According to rapper 50 Cent (Curtis James Jackson III), actor Laurence Fishburne did not like Tupac "because Tupac was so much smarter than everyone around him. He [Fishburne] said he didn't like the way Tupac behaved because he knew that Tupac knew better. I understood what he meant."[99] Fishburne believed Tupac should have been smart enough not to do things that endangered his reputation and his life, like using drugs, and more careful about whom he associated with.

Many people, however, defend Tupac against the charges levied by his detractors.

Tupac's Admirers

Kevin Powell is a black journalist who knew Tupac quite well. He argues that Tupac's lifestyle and the views he expressed in his songs and poems were a powerful protest against the way a society dominated by whites treats blacks. Said Powell: "Tupac's life was an exacting sort of revenge, on white people, on snobby black people, on the rich, on anyone who had no sympathy for the oppressed and voiceless on this planet."[100]

However, Afeni Shakur, who has passionately guarded her son's legacy, believes that Tupac was more than a voice of rebellion and constructive criticism. She says, "The public's fascination with

Despite his critics, Tupac Shakur earned the respect of many in the entertainment community, including famed music producer Quincy Jones, pictured.

Tupac has to do with his having risen from a life of adversity into a global icon. They identify with my son and it gives them the inspiration they so need to rise above their own hardships."[101] An example of her son's global reach came in 1998 when members of the Revolutionary United Front fighting in Sierra Leone's civil war in Africa adopted Tupac T-shirts as their official uniform. They did it because they admired his toughness and revolutionary spirit.

Famed musician and composer Quincy Jones is from an earlier musical generation, but he admires rap and has used it in his recent works. Jones knew Tupac well because his daughter, Kidada, was engaged to the rapper when he died. Jones thought that Tupac was very talented: "Tupac struck me with the power of his music, the sheer breadth of his potential talent, and his warrior spirit. Tupac's life embodied the spirit of hip hop, the music of America's youth."[102]

Jones mourns Tupac's violent death at the age of twenty-five as a tragedy that occurs all too often among young black males. He also mourns that death because it meant that Tupac was never able to reach his full potential as a musician or as a human being.

Tupac's Life Was Too Short

In 2006, on the tenth anniversary of Tupac's death, the question of what Tupac might have become and accomplished was pondered by one of his fans—Brandon Hudson, an aspiring hip-hop artist and May 2006 graduate of Duke University. According to Hudson, no one will ever know what Tupac's death meant for the world's future:

Tupac had all the potential to make a positive impact on American culture. Whatever he could've been, hip-hop has missed the positive potential he might have brought to it. One of my favorite lyrics of his is from "The Ghetto Gospel": 'If I upset you, don't stress / Never forget that God isn't finished with me yet.' I think that kind of sums him up very well.[103]

Introduction: More than a Rapper

1. Tupac Amaru Shakur, *The Rose That Grew from Concrete*. New York: Pocket, 1999, p. 3.
2. Quoted in Jacob Hoye and Karolyn Ali, eds., *Tupac: Resurrection 1971–1996*. New York: Atria, 2003, p. 247.
3. Afeni Shakur, preface, in Shakur, *The Rose That Grew from Concrete*, p. xii.
4. Quoted in Hoye and Ali, *Tupac: Resurrection*, p. 70.

Chapter 1: Tupac Shakur's Revolutionary Heritage

5. Quoted in Candace Sandy and Dawn Marie Daniels, *How Long Will They Mourn Me? The Life and Legacy of Tupac Shakur*. New York: Ballantine, 2006, p. 1.
6. Quoted in Jamal Joseph, *Tupac Shakur Legacy*. New York: Atria, 2006, p. 8.
7. Quoted in Peter Carlson, "The Gangsta Rapper's Radical Mama." *Washington Post*, September 23, 2003, p. C1.
8. Quoted in Joseph, *Tupac Shakur Legacy*, p. 11.
9. Quoted in Armond White, *Rebel for the Hell of It: The Life of Tupac Shakur*. New York: Thunder's Mouth, 1997, p. 6.
10. Quoted in Hoye and Ali, *Tupac: Resurrection*, pp. 26–27.
11. Quoted in Veronica Chambers, "Conversations with Tupac," *Esquire*, December 1996, p. 84.
12. Quoted in Joseph, *Tupac Shakur Legacy*, p. 18.
13. Shakur, *The Rose That Grew from Concrete*, p. 89.
14. Quoted in White, *Rebel for the Hell of It*, p. 15.
15. Quoted in Hoye and Ali, *Tupac: Resurrection*, p. 54.
16. Quoted in Peter Castro, "All Eyes on Her," *People*, December 1, 1997, p. 152.

17. Quoted in Jasmine Guy, *Afeni Shakur: Evolution of a Revolutionary*. New York: Atria, 2004, p. 131.

18. Quoted in VIBE, *Tupac Amaru Shakur: 1971–1996*. New York: Three Rivers, 1998, p. 15.

Chapter 2: *2Pacalypse Now* Hits the World

19. Quoted in VIBE, *Tupac Amaru Shakur*, p. 27.

20. Quoted in Hoye and Ali, *Tupac: Resurrection*, p. 64.

21. Quoted in "Tupac Shakur Speaks." Interviews on a CD accompanying the book *Tupac Shakur Legacy* by Jamal Joseph. New York: Atria, 2006.

22. Quoted in VIBE, *Tupac Amaru Shakur*, p. 28.

23. Quoted in Hoye and Ali, *Tupac: Resurrection*, p. 69.

24. Quoted in VIBE, *Tupac Amaru Shakur*, p. 27.

25. Quoted in Shakur, *The Rose That Grew from Concrete*, p. xix.

26. Tupac Shakur, "Same Song," SeekLyrics. www.seeklyrics.com/lyrics/2pac/Same-Song.html.

27. Quoted in VIBE, *Tupac Amaru Shakur*, p. 29.

28. Quoted in "Tupac Shakur Speaks."

29. Tupac Shakur, "Brenda's Got a Baby," A–Z Lyrics Universe. www.azlyrics.com/lyrics/2pac/brendasgotababy.html.

30. Quoted in Hoye and Ali, *Tupac: Resurrection*, p. 70.

31. Quoted in VIBE, *Tupac Amaru Shakur*, p. 27.

32. Quoted in Hoye and Ali, *Tupac: Resurrection*, p. 73.

Chapter 3: Tupac Becomes a Superstar

33. Quoted in Joseph, *Tupac Shakur Legacy*, p. 30.

34. Quoted in Hoye and Ali, *Tupac: Resurrection*, p. 122.

35. Quoted in Richard Corliss, "Retiring Was Not an Option," *Time*, November 24, 2003, p. 36.

36. Tupac Shakur, "Soulja's Story." SeekLyrics. www.seeklyrics.com/album/lyrics//2pac/Soulja's-Story.html.

37. Quoted in White, *Rebel for the Hell of It*, p. 78.

38. Quoted in Dennis R. Martin, "The Music of Murder." Academy of Criminal Justice Sciences. www.axt.org.uk/Hate Music/Rappin.html.

39. Tupac Shakur, "Bury Me a G," A–Z Lyrics Universe. www.azlyrics.com/lyrics/2pac/burymeag.html.

40. Tupac Shakur, "Cradle to the Grave," A–Z Lyrics Universe. www.azlyrics.com/lyrics/2pac/cradletothegrave.html.

41. Shakur, "Bury Me a G."

42. Quoted in Hoye and Ali, *Tupac: Resurrection*, p. 132.

43. Tupac Shakur, "Keep Ya Head Up," SeekLyrics. www.seeklyrics.com/lyrics/2pac/Keep-Ya-Head-Up.html.

44. Tupac Shakur, "Dear Mama," *All Eyez on Me*. www.alleyezonme.com/lyrics/2pac/0054/Dear_Mama.phtml.

45. John McWhorter, "Something 2 Die 4?" *New Republic*, November 22, 2001, p. 35.

46. Quoted in Sandy and Daniels, *How Long Will They Mourn Me?*, p. 75.

47. Quoted in Benjamin Svetkey, "Crying Foul: Tupac Shakur, Gangsta Film Star, Wants You to Know One Thing: He's Getting a Bad Rap," *Entertainment Weekly*, April 8, 1994, p. 26.

48. Quoted in Hoye and Ali, *Tupac: Resurrection*, p. 101.

49. Quoted in White, *Rebel for the Hell of It*, p. 160.

50. Quoted in Shakur, *The Rose That Grew from Concrete*, p. xv.

Chapter 4: The "Thug Life" of Tupac Shakur

51. Quoted in VIBE, *Tupac Amaru Shakur*, p. 80.

52. Quoted in Svetkey, "Crying Foul," p. 25.

53. Quoted in Hoye and Ali, *Tupac Resurrection*, p. 80.

54. Quoted in Allison Samuels and John Leland, "Trouble Man," *Newsweek*, September 23, 1996, p. 68.

55. Quoted in White, *Rebel for the Hell of It*, p. xx.

56. Quoted in Abiola Sinclair, "Tupac Tied to Murder?" *New York Amsterdam News*, January 1, 1994, p. 1.

57. Quoted in Joseph, *Tupac Shakur Legacy*, p. 33.

58. Quoted in Sandy and Daniels, *How Long Will They Mourn Me?* p. 47.

59. Quoted in Raquel Cepeda, ed., *"And It Don't Stop": The Best American Hip-Hop Journalism of the Last 25 Years.* New York: Faber and Faber, 2004, p. 142.

60. Quoted in Hoye and Ali, *Tupac: Resurrection*, p. 141.

61. Quoted in Sandy and Daniels, *How Long Will They Mourn Me?* p. 56.

62. Quoted in Hoye and Ali, *Tupac: Resurrection*, p. 155.

63. Quoted in Joseph, *Tupac Shakur Legacy*, p. 43.

64. Quoted in VIBE, *Tupac Amaru Shakur*, p. 45.

65. Quoted in Hoye and Ali, *Tupac: Resurrection*, p. 177.

Chapter 5: The Mysterious Murder of Tupac Shakur

66. Quoted in Chuck Philips, "Media Got It Wrong, He Says," *Milwaukee Journal Sentinel*, October 29, 1995, p. A8.

67. Quoted in VIBE, *Tupac Amaru Shakur*, p. 45.

68. Quoted in Hoye and Ali, *Tupac: Resurrection*, p. 134.

69. Quoted in Joseph, *Tupac Shakur Legacy*, p. 49.

70. Quoted in "Tupac Shakur Speaks."

71. Quoted in VIBE, *Tupac Amaru Shakur*, p. 108.

72. Quoted in Joseph, *Tupac Shakur Legacy*, p. 50.

73. Quoted in Sandy and Daniels, *How Long Will They Mourn Me?*, p. 86.

74. Quoted in Chambers, "Conversations with Tupac," p. 86.

75. Quoted in Kevin Powell and Joseph V. Tirella, "The Short Life and Violent Death of Tupac Shakur," *Rolling Stone*, October 31, 1996, p. 38.

76. Quoted in David Van Biema and Patrick E. Cole, "What Goes 'Round . . ." *Time*, September 23, 1996, p. 54.

77. Quoted in Samuels and Leland, "Trouble Man," p. 69.

78. Quoted in Powell and Tirella, "Short Life and Violent Death," p. 38.

79. Quoted in Chambers, "Conversations with Tupac," p. 86.

80. Quoted in Van Biema and Cole, "What Goes 'Round . . .'" p. 54.

Chapter 6: Tupac Shakur: The Immortal Rapper

81. Don McLean, "American Pie," Lyrics007.com. www.lyrics 007.com/Don%20McLean%20Lyrics/American%20Pie%20 Lyrics.html.

82. Michael Eric Dyson, "Tupac: Life Goes On," *Black Issues Book Review*, September/October 2006, p. 16.

83. Quoted in Hoye and Ali, *Tupac: Resurrection*, p. 93.

84. Quoted in Guy, *Afeni Shakur*, p. 186.

85. Quoted in Chris Bournea, "Afeni Shakur Discusses Tupac's Legacy During OSU Visit." *Call & Post*, February 9–15, 2006, p. B1.

86. Quoted in "Pac's Life," *Hip Hop Galaxy*. www.hiphop galaxy.com/2Pac-Pac-s-Life-hip-hop-4259.html.

87. Quoted in Bournea, "Afeni Shakur Discusses Tupac's Legacy," p. B1.

88. Quoted in Natasha Grant, "Tupac's 'Resurrection' on Page and Screen," *New York Amsterdam News*, November 13, 2003, p. 22.

89. Quoted in Helena de Bertadano, "My Son the Black Elvis: The First Man I Ever Liked." *The Times* (London), September 8, 2004, p. 4.

90. Quoted in Philips, "Media Got It Wrong, He Says," p. A8.

91. Dyson, "Tupac: Life Goes On," p. 16.

92. Walter Edwards, "From Poetry to Rap: The Lyrics of Tupac Shakur," *Western Journal of Black Studies 26, no. 2* (2002): 64.

93. Quoted in David Menconi, "Larger than Life: 10 Years After His Death, Tupac Shakur's Legacy Continues to Grow,"

Raleigh (NC) News & Observer, September 10, 2006, p. 12.

94. Quoted in David E. Thigpen, "Tupac Is in the Building," *Time*, April 16, 2001, p. 56.

95. Quoted in Carlson, "The Gangsta Rapper's Radical Mama," p. C1.

Epilogue: Should Tupac Shakur Be a Role Model?

96. Quoted in McWhorter, "Something 2 Die 4?," p. 31.

97. Michael Medved, "Glorification of Rapper Shakur Degrades African-Americans," *USA Today*, November 19, 2002, p. A21.

98. McWhorter, "Something 2 Die 4?," p. 35.

99. 50 Cent, "Tupac Shakur: The Immortals," *Rolling Stone*, April 21, 2005, p. 94.

100. Kevin Powell, *Who's Gonna Take the Weight? Manhood, Race, and Power in America*. New York: Three Rivers, 2003, p. 187.

101. Quoted in Grant, "Tupac's 'Resurrection' on Page and Screen," p. 22.

102. Quoted in VIBE, *Tupac Amaru Shakur*, p. 13.

103. Quoted in Menconi, "Larger than Life," p. 12.

June 16, 1971

Tupac Amaru Shakur is born in New York.

June 1986

Tupac and his family move to Baltimore, Maryland.

June 1988

Tupac and his family move to Marin City, California.

January 3, 1991

Tupac makes his recording debut on a Digital Underground album.

November 12, 1991

2Pacalypse Now, his first album, is released.

January 17, 1992

Tupac stars as Bishop in the movie *Juice*.

August 22, 1992

A six-year-old boy is shot to death in Marin City during a fight between members of Tupac's entourage and others.

July 23, 1993

Poetic Justice, a movie starring Tupac and Janet Jackson, is released.

October 31, 1993

Tupac is arrested for allegedly shooting two off-duty Atlanta police officers; the charges are later dropped.

November 18, 1993

Ayanna Jackson claims that Tupac and three other men sexually assaulted her in a hotel room.

March 23, 1994

Tupac stars as Birdie in the movie *Above the Rim*.

November 30, 1994

Tupac is shot five times and robbed of $40,000 worth of jewelry in the lobby of a New York recording studio.

December 1, 1994

A jury acquits Tupac of sodomy and weapons charges but finds him guilty of sexual abuse in the Jackson case.

February 14, 1995

Tupac is sentenced to one-and-a-half to four-and-a-half years in prison for sexual abuse.

April 1, 1995

While Tupac is in prison, his third album, *Me Against the World*, debuts at number one on Billboard's pop chart.

October 13, 1995

Tupac is freed on bail from prison.

February 13, 1996

Tupac releases *All Eyez on Me*, the first double CD by a rapper.

September 7, 1996

Tupac is shot after leaving the Mike Tyson–Bruce Seldon fight in Las Vegas.

September 13, 1996

Tupac dies of his wounds at the age of twenty-five.

For Further Exploration

Books

Debi Fee, ed., *2pac: A Photo Tribute*. Los Angeles: Ashley Communications, 1996. This book has interesting photographs of the late rapper.

Heather Forkos, *Tupac Shakur*. Philadelphia: Chelsea House, 2001. An informative biography of the rapper for young readers.

Cathy Scott, *The Killing of Tupac Shakur*. Las Vegas: Huntington, 1997. The book closely examines Tupac's murder.

Quinton Skinner. *All Eyez on Me: The Life and Time of Tupac Shakur*. New York: MTV, 2004. A biography of Tupac that focuses on his music.

Films

Tupac: Resurrection. Paramount, 112 minutes, 2003. A filmed version of Tupac Shakur's life that is narrated by the slain rapper through audio clips from his interviews.

Web Sites

All Eyez on Me (www.alleyezonme.com). This Internet site is a good source of facts, photos, and audio clips about Tupac Shakur.

Makaveli (www.makaveli-branded.com). The Internet site for Tupac Shakur's official clothing line.

Thug Life Army (www.thuglifearmy.com). This Internet site, which includes photographs and audio clips, has information on Tupac Shakur's life and his works.

Tupac Amaru Shakur Foundation (www.tasf.org/). The foundation started by Afeni Shakur provides quality training in the arts to help young people discover their creative talents.

Michael V. Uschan has written more than fifty books, including *Life of an American Soldier in Iraq*, for which he won the 2005 Council for Wisconsin Writers Juvenile Nonfiction Award. It was the second time he won the award. Mr. Uschan began his career as a writer and editor with United Press International, a wire service that provided stories to newspapers, radio, and television. Journalism is sometimes called "history in a hurry." Mr. Uschan considers writing history books a natural extension of the skills he developed in his many years as a journalist. He and his wife, Barbara, reside in the Milwaukee suburb of Franklin, Wisconsin.